THE HOBO HANDBOOK

THE HOBO HANDBOOK

A Field Guide to Living by Your Own Rules

JOSH MACK

adamsmedia
Avon, Massachusetts

Published by
Adams Media, a division of F+W Media, Inc.
57 Littlefield Street, Avon, MA 02322. U.S.A.
www.adamsmedia.com

ISBN 10: 1-4405-1227-2
ISBN 13: 978-1-4405-1227-8
eISBN 10: 1-4405-2619-2
eISBN 13: 978-1-4405-2619-0

Printed in the United States of America.

10 9 8 7 6 5 4 3 2 1

Library of Congress Cataloging-in-Publication Data
Mack, Josh.
The hobo handbook / Josh Mack.
p. cm.
ISBN 978-1-4405-1227-8
1. Tramps—United States. I. Title.
HV4505.M33 2011
305.5'68—dc22
2011010229

Certain sections of the book deal with activities that may result in serious bodily harm or even death. The authors, Adams Media, and F+W Media, Inc. do not accept liability for any injury, loss, legal consequence, or incidental or consequential damage incurred by reliance on the information or advice provided in this book. The information in this book is for entertainment purposes only.

Interior illustrations by Kurt Dolber

For Joanne

ACKNOWLEDGMENTS

To all those who had the vision and fortitude to forge their own way, often by necessity, and who have helped to foster and maintain a sense of creative spontaneity and personal freedom in a world increasingly driven by logarithms. Your impact, though so rarely acknowledged, cannot be overestimated. Personally, I am indebted to Brendan O'Neill and Wendy Simard for their endless patience, skill, and attention. Thanks for that. And finally to Alyssa, a homesteader in skill and at heart, you are the engine in my life. Bless you.

CONTENTS

Hobo Aptitude Test

WHY DO YOU WANT TO BE A HOBO? (IF IT'S FOR THE FAME AND FORTUNE, YOU'RE OUT OF LUCK)

In order to gauge your potential readiness to tackle some of what lies ahead, whether it's eating nothing but bulgur wheat for three days in the winter while waiting for a train out of Deadwater, Maine, or scrubbing latrines for a few bucks at a national park in Colorado, take a few minutes and plumb the depths of your resilience by answering the questions below.

It can't be stressed enough how dangerous hopping freight trains can be. Accidents can result in amputations and are often fatal.

You're thinking:

1. Never thought it would be otherwise. I'm like a cat. No worries.
2. I thought that might be the case. I'll check it out, talk to some people that have done it, and take it from there. If it's too crazy, I'll find another mode of transportation.
3. Whoa, that doesn't sound so good. I was hoping for something different. Don't think I'll be trying this.
4. Of course it is dangerous! What nutjob would think otherwise? I like my life the way it is.

Despite what many might think, hopping freight trains and living a hair outside of society's reach isn't a constant fast rush of excitement, bouncing from one place to another. There's a lot of waiting, for hours and even sometimes days.

You're thinking:

1. Whatever, I'm awesome at making the most of the time that I have. I can entertain myself for hours.
2. I kinda figured that. No biggie as long as I have a good book.
3. That sucks, but what're you gonna do? Can't control life.
4. There's nothing I hate more than waiting. I lose my mind just waiting in line for a cup of coffee. I think I'll find another way to get around.

A lot of the people you'll be meeting are a bit more "out there" than the people you met at the poetry slam who you thought were "out there." Most folks are good, but like anywhere—now even more so—people can be . . . "challenging."

You're thinking:

1. That's just what I'm looking for.
2. I can handle whatever comes my way.
3. Hmmm . . . I was kinda hoping not to meet anybody.
4. Forget it, just the thought creeps me out and makes me want to watch a Disney movie instead.

Dining on the road can be monotonous and a little rough around the edges.

You're thinking:

1. I'm unfazed. Food is just another word for nourishment, and tastiness is just an unnecessary luxury. I could eat peanut butter and rice cakes till the cows come home, and just rice cakes if there isn't any peanut butter; if there aren't any rice cakes, I'll eat the crumbs from the bottom of the bag, and if even those are all gone, I can always catch a grasshopper.
2. I'm not too worried. I can make do, and don't need anything too fancy. Though I'd go a little hungry before dumpster diving.
3. Well, how rough are we talking?
4. Forget it. I live for gourmet grub, and minus that there's just no reason for me to push forth.

Living the hobo lifestyle pretty much guarantees the end of steady paychecks. There is no job security, and not much opportunity for advancement. After two years of being a hobo—although you'll be a more experienced hobo—you're still a hobo. The freight cars will still be the same, and you won't get to ride a nicer one because of seniority.

You're thinking:

1. I am creating a new paradigm, and will manufacture my own advancements and will do what is needed. When the time comes, I'll make do.
2. Duh. If I had a great job and was totally happy, would I even be considering this in the first place?
3. Whatever, I don't plan on being a hobo forever, and while I am I'll make the most of the adventure and worry about a 401(k) whenever I tire of traveling—or develop a sense of mortality. Whichever comes first.
4. This whole idea sounds crazy to me.

Do you want to be a hobo or more of a freewheeling traveler for a few months? A hobo is a person whose life takes place on the road, and who earns his money by working whatever jobs come his way.

You're thinking:

1. I'm really into this. I'm tired of what I do and not looking forward to what currently lies ahead of me. I need something different.
2. I have no idea what a hobo is or does, but I want to be one.
3. An eco-tourism tour will make me feel like a hobo, right?
4. Yeah, I get what a hobo is, and if I stop and think about it, I'm not into it at all. Cabo, here I come.

Are you prepared to live your life moving from makeshift home to makeshift home, sometimes camping by the side of the railroad tracks while waiting for the next train or finding couches to crash on, and when neither is available, seeking out the best-looking ditch you can find to put up your flag?

You're thinking:

1. I can sleep anywhere, and I mean *anywhere*. Sitting, standing, lying down, in motion, still, tree roots under my back, pillow, no pillow, inside, outside—it's all the same to me.
2. I'm pretty open-minded, but sleeping in a ditch isn't something I'm planning on. Now, sleeping in a cornfield, that I can handle.
3. I am planning on taking my life on the road, but I'm thinking more along the lines of crashing on other people's couches and staying in hostels when I have to. When it comes to camping, the closest I can come is sleeping in a tent within walking distance of some campsite bathrooms and showers.
4. Dude, you're kidding me, right? Why am I reading this book?

Are you daydreaming about comfortable, scenic, and slow rides in an open boxcar that will gently rock you to sleep? Today's trains, though still trains, are a different breed from those traversing the country in the late 1800s and early 1900s. Today's trains move fast, don't make half as many stops as they used to, and pull into yards that are surrounded by security.

You're thinking:

1. Fun schmun. This is business.
2. Hey, that was then, this is now. I'll take what I can get. No rose-colored glasses on this guy.
3. As long as there's a working bathroom, I think I'll be OK.
4. If I'm not gonna be sitting on a cool train with a huge open window facing the world as we pass by herds of wild horses, my interest in all of this is pretty much less than nothing.

There's a mystique surrounding the hobo making him something akin to the lone cowboy who has to keep rambling, moving off into the sunset. The reality is more that you'll be cleaning out somebody's basement and hiding in a lot of bushes while waiting for a train.

You're thinking:

1. That's awesome!
2. Well, not quite what I was expecting, but things can't always be rocket ships and fireworks.
3. On second thought, I think I'll pass.
4. Can't say the idea ever occurred to me to put "romantic" and "hobo" in the same sentence in the first place.

Expecting a spiritual transformation along the way that that will bring you six steps farther from a Visa and one step closer to the Buddha? A few days covered in road grime without anything to sleep on but some battered cardboard might make a little help from a credit card seem to trump any gleaned wisdom from the Buddha.

You're thinking:

1. Visa, along with every other credit card, exists purely to prey on people. I will do everything possible to deny them the pleasure.
2. I'm already a Buddhist and don't blame the corporations—they're just an illusion anyway.
3. Yeah, credit cards suck, but they serve a purpose—one of them being that after a few weeks of suffering with an inestimable number of coffee grounds stuck in my teeth from drinking cowboy brew I can go into a Starbucks and order a venti soy latte with an extra shot without even a dime in my pocket. The Buddha is cool and all, but if he were in my shoes he'd order one, too.
4. What's the Buddha done for me lately? I wouldn't be standing here in my Super Fly shoes reading this today if it weren't for my credit card. No thanks.

Now take a look back and review your answer pattern:

If you answered predominantly "1s," pack your bag, because there's a train on its way; mostly "2s" and this hobo thing might be a pretty good idea for you; mostly "3s" and there are some good hobo movies you could always watch; and a few "4s" and you already know where you're at.

INTRODUCTION

The New Hobo Code

"Just in my swim shorts, barefooted, wild-haired, in the red fire dark, singing, swigging wine, spitting, jumping, running—that's the way to live. All alone and free . . ."

—JACK KEROUAC, IN *THE DHARMA BUMS*, HAVING JUST SET UP CAMP ON A BEACH AFTER A DAY RIDING A FREIGHT TRAIN.

The daily grind has ground you down and there are days when given the option of sticking pins in your eyeballs or listening to your voicemail you're not sure which way you'd lean. Each day you walk the same paths, park in the same spots, eat at the same places, stare at the same ads, and stay up late watching the same movies; you note with jealousy cars bearing out-of-state license plates. An adventure at this point, you hate to admit, is a power outage during a thunderstorm. Taking stock of your life, you marvel at the subjective rules you've become accustomed to. What's the big deal in substituting salad for fries? Why can't you serve wine in a coffee cup? Why aren't cell phone chargers universal? You wonder at a life free of bills, landlords, alarm clocks, parking tickets, the IRS, overdraft fees, and ads pushing you to choose one kind of cereal over another or promising salvation in a bottle. And a small bottle at that, given the price.

Then one day—perhaps today—after you've been on hold for twenty minutes and the automated customer service "person" is asking you to repeat your selection for the third time or press pound to return to the main menu, the obvious solution to your societal incarceration hits you: quit your job, donate your car, toss your credit cards, and become a hobo. Awestruck, you stop dead in your tracks and wonder why you didn't see it before, thinking of all the time you could have saved if a hobo had just come in to school on career day and with a wink shown you the door marked "exit."

You catch a glimpse of your possible future. Instead of the recycled air from the building's central HVAC system pushing past your face you feel the breeze coming off a stream while you pass above in a boxcar, the door wide open and the sun on the horizon torching the clouds an electric blood-orange. Now that's the life, you think to yourself, that's where I'm gonna shine.

As the euphoria starts to fade from your decision to cast off your chains and raise your freedom flag, you will undoubtedly find that some questions arise; after all, the last hobo you can remember seeing was the guy modeling a "Harry the Hobo" costume at HalloweenMart. Can you do this? If you weren't born on the backseat of a Greyhound bus are you irreparably preprogrammed for a life of car payments and resealing the driveway every three years? You've ridden the subway without incident, and as a kid your dad once took you on an Amtrak train for nostalgia's sake, but boarding a moving freight train? Can you still call home if you get lonely? And what about a paycheck? In the past whenever you've been short of change you've found yourself staring helplessly at a vending machine while feeling really thirsty. Do we still even *have* hobos roaming the country?

Although some have declared the hobo "dead," and it's true the hobo lifestyle of the turn of the century—crossing a still-wild western frontier while earning money following the harvests—has largely caught its last train, there is indeed a niche for the twenty-first-century hobo. Adaptive modern-day hobos are just as likely to find a job on Craigslist while sipping a soy latte they put on a debit card as they are to brew a pot of cowboy coffee over a small campfire by the tracks as they wait for word to arrive on where the jobs are. In addition, they may intersperse traveling by freight car with a ride on a Greyhound when that proves more efficient. Or they may not travel by freight car at all and instead rendezvous with other hobos via an Internet newsgroup on their smartphone no need to interpret chalk-drawn symbols left on a tree stump these days. However, mixing traditional hobo skills with more modern methods may very well become your de facto "new" way of life as you forge ahead on your path.

Enter *The Hobo Handbook*. This guide offers a crash course for taking your life on the road and funding it as you go. You'll learn how to set up camp, find a job, catch some food, find yourself some transport, and when the time comes, how to sleep in a ditch. You might decide after a few days that you've found your true calling, or you may say to yourself, "Well, that was . . . terrible; nine to five and a little rent once a month doesn't sound so bad, after all," and return to your regular life. But either way, you will have tried it.

A WORD ON FREIGHT-CAR HOPPING: Trespassing on railroad property and catching out on freight cars is not just illegal, but incredibly dangerous. The number of deaths and injuries over the years related to this activity is astounding (in just the ten-year period from 1929 to 1939 more than 24,000 people were killed and another 27,000 injured). We would never suggest you actually do it, and it's not the only way to travel the country without handing over the keys to your freedom.

CHAPTER 1

Getting Started

THE HOBO EVOLUTION

"Every great advance in natural knowledge has involved the absolute rejection of authority."

—ALDOUS HUXLEY

Hobos have been romanticized, caricatured, pilloried, and mythologized in both literature and pop culture since the first one hopped a train without a ticket. Norman Rockwell's 1928 cover for the *Saturday Evening Post* of the "Fleeing Hobo" depicted him pot-bellied, with his shoes untied, bindle slung over his back, a harmless buffoon making off with someone's freshly baked pie—the family dog still latched on to his behind. Red Skelton's famous character, "Freddie the Freeloader," was a clown who lived beside a garbage dump and slept in a bathtub. Neither of these characters is remotely close to resembling an actual hobo, yet stereotypes persist.

bindle: Specifically a hobo's bedroll and belongings that he carried on his back, but more generically whatever bag a hobo used to hold his stuff. Stereotypically, a small handkerchief tied to the end of a stick carried over the shoulder. If you can fit all your belongings in a wrapped handkerchief, you have achieved elite minimalist hobo status.

Red Skelton's hobo clown, "Freddie the Freeloader," typified—and reinforced—the public's perception of hobos as lazy and unemployed bums. Eternally optimistic, Freddie was always on the hunt for that which was free and easy. In one episode he breaks into a library in order to take a nap on top of the stacks, while in another he's startled awake by his alarm clock and exclaims, "Great Scott! It's Thursday! I've overslept and missed my unemployment check! Oh, well, easy come, easy go."

Today, people are more likely to identify the fifth-grade [illegible] the Halloween parade with a fake cigar and a pillow stuffed up his shirt as a hobo than a guy with a pack on his back who just walked across the railroad tracks and asked them if they knew when the next freight train was coming. Do a search for "hobo" on the Internet and you'll have to wade through a lot of high-end handbag sites and plastic clown hats, and that's before you even get to the costume and comedy sites. The true hobo is a bit harder to find.

LET THERE BE HOBOS

Where exactly did hobos come from? The first people to ride the rails and the precursors to the American hobo came about toward the end of the Civil War. According to hobo folklore, they were Erie Crip and Philly Pop, two Union soldiers. After the war they found themselves far from home, and they decided hopping a passing freight train seemed the fastest and cheapest way to get back. As one might imagine, they beat a lot of their friends home, and soon other soldiers were following suit.

With the war over, there were hundreds of thousands of men who were suddenly left with nothing to do and nowhere to be. Many had been on the road for years, leaving them with a taste for adventure; others simply had no homes to go back to. But either way, these men saw in the railroads a direct route to a new beginning. Lincoln had authorized the first transcontinental railroad in 1862 to connect the tracks in the east with those in the west, and as the tracks surged forth the soldiers went with them—riding the rails while at the same time finding work building, repairing, and maintaining them. In desperate need of a labor force that didn't mind being mobile and moving on when the job was done, the railroads were initially all too happy to provide the transportation needed (this would change). In addition to railroad work, many picked up odd jobs along the way working as farmhands and doing anthing else that would bring in money.

There is no shortage of explanations for how the term "hobo" came into being. Some say it was by combining *homeward bound boys*, a name used to describe the soldiers returning home by hopping freight trains, and *hoe boys*, given to the men who took work in the fields while riding the rails, as they were often associated with a tool of the trade. Others have suggested it came from the greeting, "Ho boy!" And others say it's from a shortening of the New York City intersection of Houston and Bowery, a common hobo hangout. Whatever the origination, "hobo" was not the word first used to describe those wandering the railways. The initial waves of homeless and purposely unemployed young men moving across the country by rail were called "tramps."

> **hobo:** A migratory worker; originated from hoe boys, the name given to the men taking work in the fields while riding the rails as they were often associated with a tool of the trade. Hobos distinguished themselves from tramps, who traveled but didn't work, and bums, who did neither.

Born of the Rail

The rails became even more populated during the depression of the 1870s by a new class of traveler: those who had lost their job in the city during the economic downturn and took to the railroads—not for adventure or excitement, but out of economic necessity. When the work dried up they moved on to the next town; some have attributed this period as marking the birth of the true hobo. These men developed annual traveling circuits that followed the growing seasons. They might be felling trees in the Pacific Northwest during the winter and harvesting wheat in Oklahoma during the summer. Others would simply follow the wheat harvest, traveling a route each year that led them from the plains of the Texas panhandle in June up to the Canadian border in August.

fruit tramp: A hobo who, yes, picked fruit to earn a living.

As time went on and their numbers grew, hobos—who previously were just individuals riding the trains in the hopes of making a buck—developed a culture of their own in a true community of migrant workers. They were people who shared the distinction of living without an address, carrying what they needed on their back, working to support themselves, and living a life free of convention. If they were proficient in a trade, they found jobs doing it. In fact, hobos have been credited with playing a major role in the development of the west—these workers moved ahead of the main population and helped lay the groundwork for the infrastructure that would soon come.

Living a hobo lifestyle might seem really romantic from a warm living room, but a better way to imagine it might be to go outside on a really cold and rainy night and sit under a tree getting soaked. If you still find it romantic, it just might be your calling. On one particularly rough night, Jack London recounts in his book *The Road*, a companion said to him while traveling, "Never again a hobo. I'm going to get a job. You'd better do the same. Nights like this make rheumatism."

WELCOME TO THE JUNGLE

While hobos lived beyond society's grasp and preferred to avoid putting down roots, not everything could be done within the confines of a boxcar. They were not hermits but active members of a community, and they sought the company of others with similar values. So while initially hobos quietly set up their own individual camps for the night, it wasn't long before things got organized. As their numbers grew, so did their camps—sometimes to an enormous size (one was once rumored to be over a mile long). These camps were known as "jungles." Here hobos could come and gather for the night and share food, stories, and information. They would learn news of other hobos as well as what traveling conditions they could expect up ahead, and in turn they could inform others about their experiences on the road.

Boxing great Jack Dempsey lived as a hobo for five years between 1911 and 1916. Traveling by rail and taking all manner of odd jobs, he changed his name to Kid Blackie. His official knockout count didn't include those he had delivered in the jungles. The sportswriter Red Smith said of him, "He was 187 pounds of unbridled violence. This isn't big by heavyweight standards, yet in the judgment of some, this black-browed product of Western mining camps and hobo jungles was the best of all pugilists."

jungle: The camps, generally in the vicinity of the railroad tracks, that hobos set up. Some were huge and essentially served as permanent hobo base camps.

Jungles sprang up throughout the country and quickly became destinations unto themselves. There were temporary jungles—where a group would stop, set up for the night, and in a day or two break it all down and move on—as well as more permanent jungles that traveling hobos could consider "home." Dinner in the jungle would often consist of "mulligan stew," made from whatever food the hobos coming into camp that night had in their pockets. Though it sounds sketchy, these stews generally earned rave reviews.

Ground Rules

Due to vagrancy laws, hobos were routinely arrested, booted out of town, and generally abused. But in a clever display of cultural prowess, they exploited a legal loophole. If you were a member of a union, you were not subject to vagrancy laws because it was assumed you were traveling for work. So hobos established their own union, Tourist Union #63. In addition, their livelihoods were dependent on people having a favorable opinion of them, and the union allowed them to distance themselves from tramps and bums.

Even a group of nine-year-olds hanging out in a tree fort knows a club needs rules if it's to function properly, and hobos were no different. They may have decided they didn't want to be bound by society's rules, but they realized that for the sake of all they couldn't just be a population of wandering contract workers hopping freight cars and practicing anarchy. In Chicago at the 1894 Annual Convention Congress of the Hobos of America (not too shabby for a bunch of drifters), they came up with governing rules.

According to their own history, in the mid 1800s a large group of hobos who had been tossed from various towns found themselves together in a jungle by the railroad tracks, and they decided something had to be done. As there were sixty-three hobos gathered, they decided upon the name Tourist Union #63 ("Tourist" perhaps being one of the early examples of marketing genius) and established an annual hobo convention. Members were issued membership cards and there was even a small office near the B&O railroad in Cincinnati, Ohio. The convention is still held to this day in Britt, Iowa, although it's now more of a hobo celebration than a serious call to order.

THE HOBO CODE OF ETHICS

1. Decide your own life; don't let another person run or rule you.
2. When in town, always respect the local law and officials, and try to be a gentleman at all times.
3. Don't take advantage of someone who is in a vulnerable situation, locals or other hobos.
4. Always try to find work, even if temporary, and always seek out jobs nobody wants. By doing so you not only help a business along, but ensure employment should you return to that town again.
5. When no employment is available, make your own work by using your added talents at crafts.
6. Do not allow yourself to become a stupid drunk and set a bad example for locals' treatment of other hobos.
7. When jungling in town, respect handouts, do not wear them out, another hobo will be coming along who will need them as bad, if not worse than you.

8. Always respect nature; do not leave garbage where you are jungling.
9. If in a community jungle, always pitch in and help.
10. Try to stay clean, and boil up wherever possible.
11. When traveling, ride your train respectfully, take no personal chances, cause no problems with the operating crew or host railroad, act like an extra crew member.
12. Do not cause problems in a train yard; another hobo will be coming along who will need passage through that yard.
13. Do not allow other hobos to molest children; expose all molesters to authorities; they are the worst garbage to infest any society.
14. Help all runaway children, and try to induce them to return home.
15. Help your fellow hobos whenever and wherever needed, you may need their help someday.
16. If present at a hobo court and you have testimony, give it. Whether for or against the accused, your voice counts!

In addition to their own lingo, hobos developed a unique system for communicating with each other out in the world via chalk-drawn symbols. These could alert fellow hobos to everything from unfriendly dogs to good places to look for work, and could be found anywhere from telephone poles to the sides of houses to sidewalks. Being cryptic, they'd only make sense to someone in the know. The numbers 2 over 10, for example, was a warning to look out for thieves, and a squiggly line told that a judge was in residence. More on these in Chapter 6.

While the code of ethics may seem dated there's an inherent message that's not: don't screw it up for the next person. You are not a rogue wandering the countryside, but a traveler whose health, safety, and well-being are dependent upon the kindness—and trust—of others. True hobos are welcoming and compassionate people looking out for one another while celebrating an unencumbered lifestyle. It is up to the individual to keep this tradition alive, and the first time you run out of water and someone says, "Here, have some of mine," you'll be happy you've built that trust.

THE HOBO UNDERGROUND

While jungles were good for a few nights camping, restive communal suppers, and the swapping of tall tales while en route to another destination, they didn't provide much in the way of infrastructure or any significant R&R. When out of work and not riding the rails, hobos developed their own urban areas within major cities that had good railroad access. Known as the "main stem," these areas were littered with cheap hotels, brothels, shops, artistic venues, and temp agencies through which hobos could land jobs all over the country (although these agencies could be exploitive and hobos sometimes referred to them as "slave markets").

The stems were where hobos could spend their "stake," the money they made while out on the road. As places where hobos were free to live their lives with little interference, stems became the birthplace of *hobohemia*, a term used to describe the resulting culture. The stems could be large, particularly during winter when jobs were scarcer. Many hobos became down and out in the stems and took to begging, or "stemming it." In the early 1990s, the stem in Chicago on West Madison Street boasted a population of some 30,000 during the summer and 60,000 during the winter. To hobos, hobohemia was a place where all was fair and well, but the public at large had a different name for it: skid row. Viewed as locations filled with homeless men, drunks, bums, crime, and businesses catering to sordid activities where no respectable person would be caught dead, regular folks deemed them places to be avoided.

stemming: When a hobo went panhandling, he was "stemming."

NOT IN MY BACKYARD

Hobos flourished from the late 1870s up until the Great Depression, but the seeds of their undoing were around from the start. The conditions that brought about the armies of homeless migrant workers of the late 1800s and early 1900s might be boiled down to war and large-scale unemployment. Groups of wandering unemployed men did not reflect well on federal or state government, and neither were communities across the country thrilled when the railroads dropped them at their doorsteps.

In 1879, Connecticut passed their Tramp Act, which not only obligated every sheriff and policeman to quickly arrest anyone suspected of being a tramp, but also offered them a reward of five dollars for every conviction. In July of 1879, an editorial in the *New York Times* began by noting, "This is the season of the year when the highways are lined with the ragged, filthy, and villainous-looking men, who slouch long the road." The author went on to describe the various tramp laws and remarked, "Next to soap and water, the tramp dreads nothing so much as work."

In a campaign whose target was pretty clear, Congress passed a series of laws between 1876 and 1886 known as the "tramp laws" that made it illegal for someone to travel looking for work without carrying money. This, of course, could make things pretty tricky given that you were traveling because you *didn't* have any money and were trying to get some. States introduced their own vagrancy laws, many sending those convicted to hard labor camps. The newspapers of the times carried editorials describing the dangerous, villainous, and malicious character of tramps. A Los Angeles paper called for the creation in California of such hard labor camps for vagrants, referring to them in the headline as "boxcar tourists" (a derogatory name at the time; not such a bad name for the "recreational" hobos of today).

Social Pressures

It didn't help the hobo's cause that while he might be asking at the front door if a family needed any help in exchange for a meal there was a tramp in the backyard running off with one of the family's chickens. An old hobo maxim, said fifty different ways, essentially boiled down to the following: Hobos traveled and worked, tramps traveled but didn't work, and bums didn't travel or work. While the public may have held a more blurred version of these distinctions—if they made any distinctions at all—hobos did not. Unfortunately for the hobo, if he happened to be between jobs and traveling with little or no money (par for the hobo course), the law viewed him as a tramp and vagrant, and he often, when caught, was sent to a labor camp.

The hobo was being hit from all sides. As the U.S. population grew and spread across the country and communities were able to provide their own labor, the need for migrant workers plummeted. In addition, as farms started to industrialize, the amount of labor required for crops such as wheat was halved, and it wasn't long before the hobo became a pariah. Things also began to change with transportation. An increase in automobile and truck traffic meant people relied less on freight trains, and consequently, train lines began cutting back on their networks. Track mileage shrank. In 1916 there were some 254,000 miles of track in the United States, a number that would drop by more than 100,000 over the course of the next seventy-five years.

Don't Build 'Em Like They Used To

And the trains themselves were changing as well. To produce the steam that powered steam locomotives, trains would need to stop at water stations located along their routes and take on water. These proved great points of access for hobos, who would often locate their jungles in the same areas. By the late 1930s, however, diesel-powered locomotives began replacing the steam engines, eliminating the need to stop for water and enabling trains to travel long distances without stopping. Diesel trains also moved with greater speed than their steam counterparts, and this upped the difficulty—as well as the danger—of boarding them while in motion. The hobo-friendly boxcar was also becoming scarce as a surge of newer cars—among them container cars with no entrance points—began to populate the rails.

D-Day

Yet another imposing force bore down on the hobo lifestyle, and that was FDR and his New Deal. In order to prevent a recurrence of the massive transient population that developed after the earlier depressions of the 1870s and 1890s, FDR instituted massive social programs during the Great Depression aimed at putting people to work and created unemployment insurance and transient camps where people were housed near large public works projects. The programs absorbed large numbers of the unemployed population, and unemployment insurance put a damper on the incentive to bust your butt hopping around the country where there was no guarantee of a paycheck in the first place.

But perhaps the final blow to knock the hobo population down was the beginning of World War II, when the military-industrial machine sucked up all available manpower and essentially brought unemployment to zero. Fearing the country might experience another massive hobo population that would take to the road when soldiers returned from the war, the government created the GI bill—an incredibly successful method of keeping young men out of trouble, in school, and off of the rails.

THE NEXT GENERATION

Hobos did not completely disappear, however. Though fewer in number, there were still people who refused to settle down and who saw the railroads as providing an unparalleled opportunity for a nomadic life of adventure. They took to the rails with renewed dedication to lead a life of their own choosing, working when they had to, and keeping hobo traditions alive. Where once people took to hopping freight trains as their only mode of transport, people were now hopping them to escape the "machine." Instead of the hundreds of thousands of hobos once traveling on the railroads, the community of hobos became much more intimate. Mention another hobo's name around a campfire in a jungle and most likely others would know him—and his whereabouts. Word could spread fast.

In the fifties and sixties, the Beat Generation took a piece of the rails as their own, adding an intellectual and spiritual twist to the American romance with the railroad that made hoboing somewhat of a rite of passage. By the seventies and eighties, three fairly distinct groups hopped freight cars: migrant workers made up the largest group (like the original hobos, they traveled the country following the harvests), followed by modern-day tramps, simply traveling and bumming. Finally, there were the "yuppie," or "recreational," hobos. These people had homes, families, gardens, jobs, and seats on the local PTA, but they took to the rails for a few weeks or for a few months as a vacation from their "regular" life. By the 1990s, this newest wave of hobos was organizing over the Internet and employing modern means to listen in on the rail yards to pinpoint freight car positions and destinations.

Should you choose to abandon your current situation and join the hobo lifestyle, this eclectic mix might be counted among your new group of friends.

TAKING THE PLUNGE

But let's back up a bit. Before you quit your job, break your lease, and give your car (or skateboard) to your kid sister, take time to consider what you're getting into, or you may find yourself asking for each of them back sooner than you'd planned. (Take the Hobo Aptitude Test earlier in the book to test your readiness to hit the road.) Absolute freedom doesn't come with heated seats and cruise control—or much of a benefits package. As far as get-rich-quick schemes go, ditching your regular life and becoming a hobo ranks pretty low, coming in just above knitting finger puppets in your basement. And traveling under the radar can leave you vulnerable—physically, mentally, financially, and legally.

Your Physical Limits

Hitchhiking and hopping freight trains *will* compromise your safety, so don't think you carry some sort of invisible safety shield that will inoculate you from the dangers. Furthermore, even when you're not in danger, it will get really uncomfortable at times—and we're not talking when you were a kid and had to sleep on the floor while visiting your Uncle Harry kind of uncomfortable or the ski lift stopped moving for fifteen minutes and it sure was cold up there kind of uncomfortable. James Michener once described his years as a hobo as "years of wonder and enchantment." But for every Michener you can bet there were thirty hungry freezing guys out there with wet shoes and socks who would have given their last penny to be in a bed with clean sheets and the promise of breakfast the next morning. Make sure you don't adopt a holier-than-thou attitude, proudly announcing to your family and friends that you no longer have a need for all of this false, capitalist-inspired manufactured reality and that they, too, should stop drinking the Kool-Aid, only to return a week later after you discover a tick in your sleeping bag.

Check Your Head

Then there's the spiritual matter. People have different ways of handling their worries that life is passing them by or that they have been sleeping giants of untapped potential for far too long. Some join an ashram, others start running marathons, some start volunteering, and others bite the bullet and finally read *War and Peace*. You may be feeling the same way. But remember the old adage: Wherever you go, there you are. You will still be looking up at the same clouds as all the homeowners and apartment dwellers you left behind, you'll still have your same allergies, and if you didn't love writing poetry before, you're probably not going to have an epiphany riding freight cars that will make you start.

You will undoubtedly experience moments when you suddenly "see" and become convinced you've just cracked society's ever-elusive master code, but your every waking moment will not be spiked with phenomenal bursts of enlightenment. Instead, a fair amount of your time will be spent contemplating mundane things like wondering where you can brush your teeth, if this toilet paper is biodegradable, how to keep from being seen behind this bush, and whether you smell okay enough to have lunch in a café.

Ask yourself why you're considering a nomadic life in the first place. Do you really need to go through with this, or would a weekend in the Sierras suffice? If you know you're craving something more than a weekend camping trip without a cell phone and that emptying your closet of a few extra sweaters and throwing out all the arts and crafts you made in grade school will not provide enough simplification for you, it may indeed be time to haul anchor.

The Ride Might Be Free, but Life Isn't

Unless you have a plush bank account or a patron saint willing to wire you money when you tire of foraging, you're going to need to support yourself. You can do this anyway you can. You don't have to travel from town to town looking for hard labor. Make your living as a writer? Bring your laptop and continue doing what you do. Web designer? The same applies. Many home-based businesses can also be brought along on the road. Free wireless Internet is becoming ubiquitous, and there are even a growing number of cities that offer free Wi-Fi in such places as public libraries and parks.

There are no hard and fast rules about how to do this. The idea is that you are making your own way and creating your own lifestyle for however long you want to, and the whole premise of your adventure is that you are now free from social pressure to conform. You don't need to travel back in time and live like it's 1929 to feel unfettered, and traveling with a laptop does not make you a slave to the man; if it makes you feel better, slap a subversive sticker on it.

Am I an Outlaw?

If you're hopping freight trains and trespassing on railroad property, yes, you are. Not quite in the same league as Jesse James, but your method of transport does put you on the wrong side of the law. Still, you're getting in at a good time: chain gangs, labor camps, and deportation to the state line are no longer the preferred forms of punishment—unless you cause excessive damage or a derailment, it's a misdemeanor and most likely you'll just get a ticket. If you are given a ticket, however, and don't appear in court thinking it'll never catch up with you, don't plan on getting in any trouble in that state should you revisit. Nothing is so disheartening as getting pulled over a few years later for a broken taillight and discovering there's a warrant for your arrest.

Bear in mind that you don't live in 1892. There are plenty of other ways to travel these days—and legally—while still living on the road and practicing a new and independent lifestyle. More on this in Chapter 3.

REMEMBER: Hobos came about toward the end of the American Civil War, initially composed of road-hardened war veterans and later those looking for work during the economic depressions of the late 1800s and early 1900s. Though often romanticized—and you will have those idyllic moments—a hobo lifestyle can be pretty gritty. Don't jump in expecting a cakewalk.

Did You Know James Michener Hoboed?

James Michener was born in 1907 and is mostly known for his books, most of them about places (at some point or another, you may have seen a row of books with names of different states and countries for titles and wondered what that was all about). But he didn't just write about places, he visited them, and by the time he was twenty he had already toured the majority of the country either by hitchhiking or hopping freight trains. Interviewed in the documentary "American Hobo," Michener says, "I rode the rods from Iowa to Illinois and a more hellish experience no young fellow ever had. *It was horrible*. You set up a little protection there to keep the soot out of your face, and you bounced along. And you felt the ride would never end. It was a descent into Hell. And how these men could do it again and again and again bewildered me."

In his aptly titled autobiography, *The World Is My Home*, he talks about his decision to leave his home in his teens by hitchhiking west: "I saw that mysterious road outside my house, the eastern part leading to a dead end, the western worlds unknown, I was determined to explore the latter." And so he left, working for carnivals and doing other odd jobs along the way.

Over the years, Michener never strayed too far from his down-to-earth roots, seeing himself as no different from anyone else. He had disdain for being described as an "author," feeling that it stunk of pomposity, and despite making millions (most of which he donated), he never bought shaving cream. Why? Because he'd learned early on that he could use leftover bits of soap instead. Toward the end of his life he still yearned for the open road, and told the *Hobo Times* that he was "still a bum at heart. I long to hit the road again to go anywhere on any project, but alas, I've been hit by a troublesome health problem which keeps me tied to one spot, but in memory I travel everywhere."

CHAPTER 2

Getting Ready

TRAVELING LIGHT OR HEAVY

"Simplicity is making the journey of this life with just baggage enough."

—AMERICAN WRITER
CHARLES DUDLEY WARNER

So if you choose to try out the hobo lifestyle, where do you start? Throw a toothbrush and a change of clothing in a bag, wander down to the nearest railroad crossing, and chase the first train that comes along? Only if you want the first day of your liberation to end with the headline, "Man quits job—wants it back." You need to prepare, study up, and plan ahead.

Most people are creatures of habit, and while you're about to lose most of yours, a lot will depend on the kind of hobo you choose to be. This is kind of like your "choose your own adventure" moment. If you want to be a complete minimalist, you can head out with little more than a blanket, learn what types of berries are edible, and grow your hair long. Alternatively, you could choose to head out carrying the latest in high-tech traveling gear with the intention of being your very own Swiss Army knife.

THE MINIMALIST

Traveling with the bare minimum gives you a low overhead. Your pack will be wondrously light, and you'll be secure in the knowledge that everything you currently own would fit in your old sock drawer (the fact that you once had enough socks to fill an entire drawer may soon strike you as excessive). If you're making your way with just the bare essentials, you will pretty much have to survive on pocket change, pooling resources with other travelers you meet, your wits, and a steadfast determination (after all, if they did it this way before, you should be able to do it now, right?).

This kind of hobo was described by Jack Kerouac in *The Vanishing American Hobo* as having "two watches you can't buy in Tiffany's, on one wrist the sun, on the other wrist the moon, both bands are made of sky." In the best of times you might find yourself feeling like Huck Finn, rolling down the river without a care in the world and a corncob pipe tucked behind your ear while you keel over belly laughing over tall tales with your trusted traveling companion. Granted, you could also end up alone in the rain at two in the morning near a rail yard with no place to stay, nothing to eat, and cold air blowing through a gaping hole in the crotch of your only pair of pants. But so it goes, you'll tell yourself . . . or someone else surely will.

With a light load, you can move more quickly and have a higher probability of eluding a ticket—or worse—from the railroad police. Likewise, your evasive maneuvers unencumbered, you have a greater chance of escaping a less-than-friendly fellow traveler whose path you may cross—although you probably won't be an attractive target as one look at you and your bag and thieves will decide you can keep whatever slim pickings you have. It's the ruggedized laptop and the $50 headlamp that draws unwanted admirers.

As a teenager, former Russian president Boris Yeltsin traveled Russia by rail while working odd jobs. Riding on a train car roof, he once got into a card game with some nefarious individuals and proceeded to lose all of his clothes with the exception of his underwear. One more loss at cards meant he'd be thrown from the train. The incentive to save his life must have bettered his card playing, because instead he won back his clothes.

As a minimalist, you also don't have to worry about being obsessively careful with your pack. After all, when the most valuable thing you're carrying is a T-shirt, launching your bag into a boxcar or tossing it into the back of a pickup isn't much cause for concern. And if in some unfortunate event you happen to lose your bag, it's not much of a setback; a quick stop at the local Salvation Army and you can be back up and running in no time. Indeed, traveling light means you cast off all that once weighed you down—perhaps including a toothbrush should it get covered in mud because you weren't carrying any Ziploc bags to keep it safe.

READY FOR ANYTHING

Alternatively, you can choose to be the quintessential twenty-first-century hobo, outfitted with a laptop, energy bars, and clothing specifically designed for rugged adventure and tailored to the particular season in which you're traveling. Instead of following a compass you made from a leaf and a paper clip in a shallow pool of water, you'll Google your directions. And rather than hopping some mysterious freight train, you might catch a ride with someone you found on Craigslist who happens to be driving in your direction. Now you're a "rubber tramp."

rubber tramp (or tire tramp): A hobo traveling by means other than the rails, whether by car, truck, or motorcycle—anything with rubber wheels. It's not in itself derogatory.

Jungles are nowhere near as common as they were in the heyday of the hobo, and so your chances of finding a well-equipped camp with pots and pans are not what they used to be. Being well equipped yourself can help make up the difference and make your traveling experience significantly easier on the body. You'll be that much more self-sufficient if you're out there with a tent, additional clothes, a small cook stove, and the supplies to last a few days or more on your own.

Not Just a Mooch

But it's not just "out there" that having the gear you need is helpful. As a self-contained traveling one-person show, you want to be able to do the most you can without requiring any sacrifice from those around you. When you're offered a place to stay for the night, it's great when you can politely refuse offers of a towel, blankets, food, or use of their computer with an easy, "That's great, thanks, but I'm all set." When people feel it's not any kind of imposition to have you around, you up your chances of getting a few more nights out of it and maybe even a good referral down the line.

If you happen to have a trade that you're good at, you'll stand a better chance of getting a job—and higher pay as well—if you're able to carry some of the tools you'll need. If you have good carpentry skills, try bringing your tool belt along. Got some electrical skills? Bring some critical hand tools along with you. These can be great in a pinch if you happen to bump into someone with a problem you can easily solve. Every buck counts.

This approach can leave you feeling a lot more comfortable in general and pretty much ready for anything, but you'll experience the downside as your attempt to move effortlessly across the country is weighed down by a 75-pound pack (if that seems absurd, consider that there are hobos who actually travel with 100-pound packs!). A heavy but well-fit pack, however, can be easier to carry than a lighter, but poorly fit pack. If you can afford it, get a pack specifically designed for someone your size. If you can't, and have to rely on whatever you can get your hands on, grin and bear it. It'll build character.

YOUR MODERN-DAY BINDLE

One of the most enduring characteristics people associate with the hobo is the "bindle," the little sack attached to the end of a stick the hobo carried over his shoulder. You are not going to take a bandana and stuff it with your sleeping bag, some books to read, and a few pounds of food and then tie it up real nice and carry it around on a stick. And rest assured, neither did they. What was more common for the hobo was to wrap his extra clothes and personal belongings up in his bedroll, which he would then tie to his back. You could do the same. Or you could take a different approach.

Bag Styles

External-frame packs are essentially a bag attached to a frame. The advantage with these is that much like the roof of a car versus its trunk, you can attach a lot more than would fit inside. Also, if need be, you can dispense with the manufacturer's bag and attach your belongings to it in any way you see fit given your immediate needs. If you have several large items that won't fit in a pack but can be bundled, this might be for you.

Internal-frame packs are bags in which the frame is built into the fabric. As opposed to external frames, these bags are more ergonomic and will fit tightly to the contours of your body. Packed well you'll feel as if you're carrying one big item on your back as opposed to several. And if you are traveling with a few items that won't fit in the main cargo pocket, most of these come with a number of areas where you can lash items to the outside of the pack.

Then there are the bags you just sling over your back and carry any way you can like duffel bags, gym bags, and standard backpacks. There are several disadvantages to these: With the exception of the regular backpack you won't have both hands free, they don't carry as well since the weight isn't evenly distributed throughout the bag and on your body, and—we've all been there—trying to squeeze the two sides of a bag together while quickly trying to zip it closed is a pain. While nowhere near as easy if you have a lot of gear (one of these at eighty pounds will wear you down fast—not to mention the straps will cut off the circulation in your hands), if you're traveling with the bare minimum, they can work.

If the straps on the duffel bags are long enough, it's possible to use them as backpacks but be prepared for hard and irregular objects to jab you in the back. For the first twenty seconds this may be bearable, but in half an hour it can seem like these objects are actively trying to tunnel through your back. Still, you can be sure those riding the rails during the Great Depression didn't stop off at REI for the perfect bag before heading to the train yards.

HOW TO FIT YOUR PACK

Here's how to fit your pack:

1. First you'll need to measure your torso. While tilting your head forward, feel for the largest bony point at the base of your neck right above your shoulders. That will be one end of the measurement. Next, grab your hip bones with your thumbs pointing behind your back and toward each other. Have a friend measure from the bony point down to the middle of the horizontal line that would be made if your thumbs were super long and able to touch each other. Bag sizes are based on torso length, and now you know yours. Get the one that fits.
2. With the right bag, now you need to adjust the shoulder strap height. First (with your gear already in) put the pack on and tighten the hip belt until it's snug. You want the straps to be resting comfortably on your shoulders, not supporting the weight of the pack—your hips should be doing that. If your shoulder straps are handling the weight, the straps are set too low and you'll be doing a lot more work than you need to be. Take the pack off and raise the straps.

WHAT—AND HOW—TO PACK

Here's a complete rundown of things to consider when you pull your bag together—whether you go minimalist or go big.

THE ESSENTIALS

* Water bottles
* Some big contractor garbage bags, the 3 ml thickness type. These are especially useful to put over an external frame pack in rough weather, and make great waterproof seats when the ground is wet.
* Ear plugs. If you end up riding the rails, you'll fall in love with them. And you may not always be sleeping in the quietest places, so once again, you'll fall in love with them.
* Multipurpose knife and tool combo, e.g., Leatherman, Swiss Army knife, etc.
* Weatherproof backpack
* Toothbrush. (And instead of toothpaste, consider keeping a small sack of baking powder. You can brush your teeth with it, it's great for saving burned cooking pans, and you can use it to deodorize stinky shoes—which you'll probably get.)
* Multivitamins
* Atlas and rail map
* Means of illumination, preferably a headlamp
* Sleeping bag and compression sack to keep it in. (You'll be amazed how small your sleeping bag can get.)
* Layers of clothing, preferably wool and synthetic materials, which will dry quickly, as opposed to cotton, which takes forever to dry.
* Underwear. Leave your tighty whities and bulky boxers at home. Instead, get a couple pairs of lightweight, fast-drying briefs made with moisture-wicking material. Super easy to wash, and with a few good wrings they'll be dry in no time.

* Three or four pairs of socks, wool or synthetic.
* Set of dark clothes to elude the "bulls" in the train yard, as well as steering clear of the Freight Train Riders of America (FTRA), a not always so friendly gang of rail riders.

bull: A member of the railroad police. Hobos have had a cat and mouse game with the bulls for over a hundred years.

* Set of clothes you'll keep clean for venturing into civilization and applying for jobs (and perhaps even wearing on a date). Among hobos these are referred to as "glad rags."
* Small sewing kit. Even if you say to yourself that you have no idea how to sew, you'd be impressed what a quick learner you become when the button on your pants pops off.
* Large Ziploc-style bags. These are ridiculously helpful for keeping things organized in your pack and for protecting items from the elements. Also, it's no fun when your liquid soap pops open and saturates everything you own.
* Dr. Bronner's or something like it. You can bathe, wash your clothes, and brush your teeth with it (which will work but is a little nasty—one drop is enough).
* Water purification tablets. You've probably taken clean water for granted for most of your life, but you will be surprised at how scarce it can be when you can't find a faucet.
* Travel towel. The better-quality ones absorb up to eight times their weight in liquid, and 90 percent of the water can be wrung out, making it dry at about warp speed compared to your typical household bath towels.
* Metal cup/bowl you can put over a fire. That Starbucks travel mug may look snazzy, but when the rubber starts to melt . . .
* Hat, to keep the sun out of your eyes and off your face.

* Rain poncho
* Tarp, great for putting down under your sleeping gear at night or for helping to make temporary shelter.

BONUS GEAR (COMPLETELY OPTIONAL)

* Tent and/or bivy sack
* If you plan to camp in bear country, make sure you have enough rope to hang a bear bag—about forty feet.
* Camping stove
* Cookware
* If you imagine yourself hunting for wild plants and berries to eat, make sure you bring a book on identifying which are edible. Make sure it has good pictures, not just descriptions.
* Hammock. This can turn a regular day into something bordering on ridiculously insanely awesome in just a few minutes.

First Aid Kit

Of course, no pack is complete without some kind of first aid kit. If you're sticking to urban areas you'll probably never be too far away from a drug store, but you should still carry some basics like Band-Aids, aspirin, and maybe some antibiotic ointment. Living a little farther out on the fringe while camping and hopping trains, however, is a different story. It doesn't take much to end up with a bad cut out there, and when all you have to clean it up is some spit and a dirty bandana, that bad cut can quickly turn into something else entirely.

FIRST AID ESSENTIALS

* Pain and fever medication (aspirin, Tylenol, etc.)
* ACE bandages

* Band-Aids
* Neosporin
* ACE bandage for sprains
* Sunblock
* Emergency Mylar blankets. They're itty bitty, but if your down bag gets wet and you're stuck in the cold, these could save your life.
* Antiseptic wipes
* Hand sanitizer
* Decongestants
* Motion sickness medication (if you're prone to motion sickness)

Packing Skills

You are going to turn yourself into a lean, mean, and self-sustainable traveling machine, and since no one else will be carrying your bags for you, don't pack as if anyone will. For each item you carry, you need to optimize weight, size, and utility. Why haul around soap, shampoo, and toothpaste when you can get one product that does it all? Learn to pack efficiently. As you go about your preparations lay out all the things you want to take. More than likely you have too much stuff, so pare it down. Then take a break for a few minutes, go do something else, and come back to pare it down again; remember, you're traveling the country—not exploring the Actic.

To maximize your space, take a tip from flight attendants who have perfected the art of living out of a bag. They use every square inch available in their suitcases by rolling—not folding—their clothes. If your bag is packed efficiently, you should be able to stick your hand in it and dig around without finding a lot of voids. Remember to store any bottles containing liquid in Ziploc bags—when you take a break and use your pack as an insta-chair, you'll be a lot happier when you open it later on and don't find your liquid soap everywhere but in its bottle.

A small bottle of hand sanitizer is a great example of one item with multiple uses. It works great for its intended purpose—to sanitize—but can also help start a fire in a pinch (it contains alcohol) and can be used for first aid. Good stuff.

Food

If you're planning on camping most of the time as you travel, you'll want to be fairly well stocked when it comes to food. If you'll only be camping occasionally and for the most part expect to be staying in hostels and on couches, carrying food won't be as important as finding places to stay; hauling around a lot of food when you're mostly eating at greasy spoons or when you're generally within walking distance of a grocery store isn't all that useful.

When it comes to carrying food, again, you want to think about what gives you the most bang for the buck—bang being calories, buck being weight. Energy bars are great for this, particularly PowerBars, which are pretty impervious to packing damage; they can be crushed and molded into just about any shape if they're still in their packaging and still be edible later. On the other end of the spectrum, you've got heavy stuff like water (which comes in at a little under eight and a half pounds per gallon) and canned food. Keep this in mind if you were thinking of living off of cheap—but cumbersome—cans of SpaghettiOs. A simple way to cut down on the weight of the food you're carrying is to hunt for your own squirrels and forage for your own berries, which on top of lightening your load has the added benefit of maximizing the dramatic content of any poetry you pen during your adventure.

Perishables aren't great to travel with, but if you're going to carry them, eat them first. That way they don't have as much time to get abused in your bag while in transit, and you'll get a chance to eat them before they spoil. You can roughly judge how perishable a food is by its water content—the more water, the quicker it'll go bad. One bonus if you're traveling during the winter, as far as perishables goes, is that if it's cold enough, your pack doubles as a minifridge.

When it comes to what kind of food you want to carry, determine whether you want to cook or not, and if you do want to cook, whether you're going to carry a stove or make a fire over which you'll cook in a pot. Consider that it may be tough to round up suitable firewood in a lot of places, not to mention that it's often illegal, really difficult if it's been raining, and a time-consuming process to get a meal in your growling belly. A camping stove is a great solution, and a "stove" in this case is not the large metal camping stove with three burners your family used to take along car camping when vacationing near the amusement park. You just want a single burner model that operates with a small fuel bottle. Some stoves can run on anything from kerosene to the unleaded gas you put (or used to put) in your car.

There are now some pretty tasty freeze-dried, or dehydrated, meals you can buy that come in a pouch. You can get them online or at most camping stores. All you need to do is open the pouch, pour in some boiling water, and you're pretty much good to go—in mere minutes you'll be sitting on a log eating Chicken a la King. Of course, meals in a pouch are not as cheap as bulk-bought trail mix, but they are a good way to make friends and take the edge off of feeling like you had to leave all creature comforts behind. On the downside, you'll need to either be near a water source or have carried water with you to eat them—eating them dry is akin to eating a handful of powdered herbs with some twigs mixed in.

FOUR-FOOTED TRAVELING COMPANIONS

If you have a dog, resist the temptation to bring him along. That sense that it will just be the two of you out there in the world, fearlessly adventuring and keeping each other company might seem awful nice, but you're going to be taking enough risks with just your own life, why risk your furry friend's life, too? Lobbing yourself into a boxcar is tough on its own, but it's a helluva lot harder with a sixty-pound pack and a sixty-pound pooch in tow. And we've all seen the movies where someone hiding from a boogeyman suddenly sneezes and chaos ensues. Well, you can't necessarily count on your dog to be a stealthy wingman at the precise moment you need him to be. For example, you might be hiding in the back of a boxcar waiting for the train to leave the yard when a bull walks by and your loyal companion decides to bark just in case you didn't know someone was approaching. Cover blown.

A dog can also make it tough to crash with strangers, who might be less inclined to take you in for the night—especially if they have a canine already that isn't down with sharing his kingdom with another Alpha dog or if someone in the household has allergies. The best bet for the health and well-being of your pooch and your own sanity is to leave your dog behind. As much as it might pain you to do so, you'll feel better knowing he's safe and sound with a friend or family member who can take good care of him while you're on the road.

SEASONAL CONSIDERATIONS AND PACKING

Deciding when to travel is going to have a big effect on what you need to pack and what you need to be prepared for; sleeping under the stars is great, but sleeping under them when it's sixty-five degrees out and you're in a minus-thirty-degree sleeping bag can take a lot of the fun out of it. Depending on the season, you're going to need different things.

Warm Months

There's nothing quite like traveling when the weather is nice. If you find yourself around lakes, ponds, and rivers you can go swimming during the heat of the day and then sit on the rocks and sun yourself like a frog (or whatever it is you'd like to sun yourself like). But while you won't need to pack long underwear, there are some things you should bring along that can exponentially improve your comfort.

Pack a wide-brimmed hat to keep the sun out of your eyes, off your face, and off the back of your neck. And unless you're angling for that leathery look so popular in years gone by, you'll want to tote some heavy-duty sunscreen as well. It may seem a little counterintuitive, but you won't necessarily stay cooler by hiking in a T-shirt. A light long-sleeved shirt can better regulate temperature (and protect your arms from sunburn). Pants with zippers on the legs that let you turn them into shorts are downright convenient. As for footwear, skip the flip-flops and keep a good pair of boots and walking shoes on hand. Flip-flops and sandals will kill your feet on long walks and can be lethal when used around train tracks. And even when not lethal, stub your toe enough times on roots and rocks, and you'll be ready to toss them in the bush.

More than a few hobos have found a bonus use for hats. Tipping your hat or taking it off while greeting people can greatly increase your chances of getting whatever it is that you're looking for. It shows a polite level of respect that you may have even without a hat, but the hat will draw attention to it.

For skeeters and black flies, bring some insect repellent containing DEET. Most recommend you don't use a repellent that contains more than 35 percent DEET or further on down the road a few bug bites may be the least of your problems. The better brands are water resistant so you won't sweat them off as quickly and they'll last longer in the rain. As most who have ever taken a walk through the woods when there's water nearby can attest, no-see-ums can be enough to make you lose your mind. They're the ones who create little swarm cyclones that seem to stay one foot in front of you no matter how far you go while their little drones fly up your nose and into your eyes, and bite you. They are from hell. Luckily, DEET works on them, too.

Heading out during the summer months you have the ability to travel lighter, so don't overburden yourself by carrying around all your winter gear as well. If you have friends or relatives that live somewhere along your route and you expect to be traveling that way again when the weather turns, see if they'd be willing to hold your stuff for you. Haven't bought your minus-thirty bag yet? Don't. Wait until you need it (but make sure you get it *before* the cold weather strikes).

Cold Months

If you've done very little camping before, trying it out for the first time in the dead of winter can be a pretty nasty introduction and leave you wishing you'd never even heard the word "hobo." It can be much more pleasant to start out in the spring, summer, or fall when you don't have to worry as much about battling the elements. If you're bringing a tent, practice setting it up several times before you leave. You'll be a lot happier if you already know the drill rather than trying to put it together for the first time as night quickly descends and the wind howls and you can't feel your fingers.

When the weather turned cold during the winter months, hobos and all the other traveling homeless liked to do what a lot of people like to do—head to warmer climates. Florida and California, in particular, were pretty concerned about this increased tourism and did what they could to stem the tide. In the mid 1930s, the mayor of Los Angeles accused other states of forbidding hobos and tramps from disembarking in their states so as to lay the problem at his feet. As a consequence, he asked that the police chief be authorized to create a police "foreign legion" to travel to the state borders and turn the "hordes" back. He felt sure that when the word was carried all the way to the East Coast, hobos would stop traveling West.

Since you'll likely be exposed to the elements a bit more than you might be used to, consider your destination. When you're riding a freight train from Chicago to Florida, it's not like getting on a plane where you kind of enter a wormhole in Detroit that spits you out in the Florida sunshine; you're going to have to make your slow way through all that cold weather that occurs in the states between. Pack accordingly.

> If you eschew the high-tech camping era of Patagonia and Marmot and instead yearn to travel retro-style, fashion yourself a warm bedroll!

WHAT YOU'LL NEED:

* Your rain poncho or tarp
* Up to three blankets (depending on the season)
* Sheet (optional)
* Rope or cinch straps

HOW TO MAKE IT:

1. Lay your poncho (or other waterproof covering/tarp) on the ground. This is key: You need to have something to insulate you from the ground below. Without it, you might have all the blankets in the world on top of you but you'll be spilling your heat into the ground below. Counterproductive.
2. Take your first blanket and lay it on your poncho, leaving about a third of the poncho exposed.
3. Now take your next blanket and place it over the exposed section of the poncho with its edge centered on the first blanket you put down.

4. If you're traveling during the winter months and anticipate the need for more blankets, continue to lay them down in the same order.
5. If you want a sheet, fold it in half and place it in the middle of the blankets.
6. Now beginning with the last blanket you put down, fold it over the sheet. Then take the blanket you put down before that and fold it over the sheet. Continue this until all blankets are folded.
7. You should now have a little cocoon of folded blankets in the middle of your waterproof cover. Fold it over the blankets.
8. If you want to be able to crash for the night without having to dig around too much in your pack, at this time you can neatly place some night clothes and toiletries on either end of the roll.
9. Starting from the bottom, begin to neatly and tightly roll up the bedroll. When you get to the top, tie the ends and middle with some rope or your cinch straps.
10. When you go to bed at night unroll your bedroll and slide in from the top. You'll be under the sheet with blankets below for padding, and above for warmth.

LAYERING

The basic two-layer method used most of the time, where you simply alter the weight and warmth of your pants, shirt, and jacket, is best forgotten unless you have no other options. In the winter months, several layers of clothing should be your goal. Based on your activity level, this will enable you to add or remove clothing to regulate your temperature. Another advantage to layering, as opposed to having fewer but heavier clothing, is that thin clothing will dry out faster if you get wet. If your one winter jacket gets soaked because the snow turns to rain and you have to hang it to dry, you'll be one cold individual hopping around in a T-shirt. Also you'll want to make sure that your pants aren't too tight, because when you put them on over your long underwear you won't be able to put anything in your pockets or bend at the knees without feeling like you're about to bust a seem. Long underwear—again synthetic material is best since it can wick moisture away from your body and keep you dry—is great because in addition to keeping you warm during the day, they're great to sleep in while you let your day clothes air out.

California blankets: Newspapers a hobo might use for bedding or to stuff in his clothes for added insulation when it's cold out. A play on it being warm enough in California that all you need is a newspaper for a blanket.

The basic gist behind the winter layering system is that if you're expecting some solid cold weather, ideally you'll have four layers: long underwear, pants and shirt, lightweight jacket such as a polar fleece, and lastly a shell of some sort that is preferably waterproof and wind resistant. If you're not into the idea of finding shelter and letting the more inclement weather pass, you might also want to consider a pair of waterproof pants.

You're going to want some footwear with a little more protection than an old pair of Converse kicks. Most likely, whether you're sticking to the railroads or hoofing it around some cities, you'll be walking—and walking a lot. All it takes is a big snowstorm followed by a little warm weather to turn trails and potholes into oceans of slush. Don't make the mistake of only carrying one pair of shoes. Not only will you be uncomfortable and at increased risk for frostbite, but your feet will become mini-ecosystems ripe for the kind of bacteria and fungus that thrive in a wet environment.

And again, avoid cotton socks; opt for either wool or synthetic. Wet cotton socks will make you miserable; they'll end up pulling off your heels and clumping up by your toes, and take forever to dry. If you're one of those people who can't stand either the weight of wool or the sometimes scratchy feel of it against your skin, synthetic material is the way to go.

Maybe all of this seems over the top and you think, "Whatever. Those Depression-era hobos didn't have GORE-TEX pants." That's true. But they also tended to either hole up in warmer climates during the winter or opted to stay put in urban areas until the weather was more amenable to traveling. If you've made a little money, you could always take this opportunity to find a dive motel in Vegas and live the high (or low) life for a bit.

If you know a building trade and are hoping to make some money with it, remember that winter can be a tough time. Most people aren't looking to have a large remodel done if it's ten below and part of the house needs to be open to the elements. In addition, due to a decreased amount of demand, builders are often forced to work for lower wages in order to compete and get the work that's available. What's more, they often need to work with a smaller crew. Not a great time to walk by a site and ask if they're hiring. Look at the kind of work you're hoping to do and then travel to places during the times when your services will have the best chances of being needed and most valued—there's no point showing up in the rainy season if you have plans to make a little cash working as an exterior housepainter.

So you know what you need, you've got your pack, you look good in the mirror wearing it, and you're almost ready to go. But where, when, and how? Read on. We'll soon take a look at your options.

▲ REMEMBER: Although you are heading out into the unknown, it's not an apocalyptic wasteland devoid of toothpaste or peanut butter. Yes, you want to be prepared, but no, you don't want to be carrying around enough that you and two other hobos could live out of your bag. Pack strategically; any item that takes the place of two or more is a score.

Did You Know Merle Haggard Hoboed?

Merle Haggard was born in 1937 in Oildale, California, just outside of Bakersfield. His family had struggled through the depression, and moved from Oklahoma to California after their farm burned down. His dad bought some land near where the Southern Pacific Railroad rolled into Bakersfield. Here, he grew up, poor, in one of what were known as "Hoover Camps"—cardboard shantytowns filled with the unemployed and migrant workers. Merle's place wasn't a cardboard shack, since both his parents had jobs—his dad worked for the Santa Fe railroad and his mom kept odd jobs—but an old boxcar that his dad converted into a home. With the railroad tracks almost in the front yard, Merle was hopping trains from an early age, even running away on one at the age of ten, and rode them fairly seriously from 1950 until 1956.

Haggard had a lot of different jobs and a lot of different run-ins with the law growing up. In one somewhat comic episode, Merle and a few buddies, drunk, decided to try and rob a café. Since they were trying to break in from the back, what they didn't know was what anyone approaching from the front would have realized: the café was open. They were picked up, and Merle was sent to San Quentin on two different sentences—one for five years and another for fifteen. He was paroled in three. While he was there, he was part of the prison's band, and was also there to see Johnny Cash perform his infamous New Year's show at the prison in 1958. (When they met again much later and Haggard reminisced about the show, Cash thought Haggard must have been in the band, and was surprised when Haggard told him, no, he'd been an inmate.)

Haggard did not have the soul-searching intellectually poetic experience on the rails that someone like Kerouac wrote about. In an NPR interview, he described a winter trip he took in a refrigerator car with two other hobos jammed into the ice compartment, "looking at each other with nothing to say." When asked what he learned from that, Haggard replied, "Take enough money to ride a bus." Which is not so different from what he did once, many years ago. Arriving on a train in Dunsmuir, it turned out a check he was owed from an earlier job had arrived at his mother's. She sent it to him through Western Union, and as soon as he got it, as he put it, he "got his butt" on a bus and "quitted that hoboing."

CHAPTER 3

Getting Going

WHERE ARE YOU GOING AND HOW WILL YOU GET THERE?

"Well, first thing is you gotta keep pace with it. If you can't run as fast as the train, it's never going to happen. One time I was trying to get on a train and I hit one of those railroad switches. It knocked me *hard*, sent me tumbling through the air backwards. It should've killed me, but I got up without a scratch."

—MERLE HAGGARD,
VANITY FAIR INTERVIEW, JULY 2010

Wherever it is you're going, you have to get there, and while it may not always be the "half the fun" you're hoping for, most likely it will be half of the adventure—if not more. From thumbing it on the freeway to hunkering down in a gondola, don't limit yourself to one form of travel. Your options are diverse; explore them.

Traveling the rails these days is not like it used to be in the golden age of the hobo. Back then the trains were running everywhere, and hopping on one—while dangerous—didn't quite require the skills of a gymnast. Trains may have been the main mode of transportation in the late nineteenth and early twentieth centuries for both people and freight traveling any great distance, but it was not something that would last. After endless mergers (BNSF, one of the largest freight railroad networks in North America, is the result of more than 400 mergers) and increased reliance on trucks and highways, the total miles of railroad available for travel has become anemic compared to what it used to be. While there are still an abundance of small local companies, today there are only five major freight companies—down from a high of 130 in the late 1930s.

FREIGHT TRAIN COMPANIES

Today the biggies are the Union Pacific (UP), the Norfolk Southern (NS), CSX, the Kansas City Southern Railway Company (KCSR), and the Burlington Northern Santa Fe (BNSF). Determining where and when to catch these trains is not like plugging in your destination and preferred travel dates into Travelocity.com. Freight trains don't carry passengers, just freight, and freight doesn't need to be made aware of when and where it's going, nor does it complain if it sits on the track for several hours—or even days.

Union Pacific is the goliath of them all and is the same company responsible for the first transcontinental railway. The Union Pacific pretty much covers the entire United States with the exception of the eastern third of the country, which the Norfolk Southern and CSX cover. The Kansas City Southern cuts a swath south from about Minnesota through Texas and down into Mexico. Like Union Pacific but smaller, the BNSF runs in the western United States.

hot shot: A train with priority freight that travels faster and stops less than ordinary freight trains.

Schedules and Routes

Each of these companies has a website where you can look up maps of the routes they service. The maps offered are far from specific, but from them you can still get the general gist of what companies will take you to what cities and what transfers you may need to make. Don't be surprised if it takes a little more than a week and up to fifteen or so train changes to make your way from one coast to the other. As for getting more specific information, you may have to swing a little cloak and dagger action. If you're a creative type, you could approach a dispatcher in the yards with an incredible story no one could possible doubt as to why you need the train schedules (since professionals traveling on important business rarely have dirty hands or carry a rucksack, be sure to leave it somewhere safe and wash up before giving your performance). You could also try calling the railroad for more specific information, but don't count on getting it. Since 9/11, increased security measures have been put in place around all rail yards.

One of the most direct ways to discover which trains are coming and going and time estimates for arrivals and departures is to befriend railroad employees. Part of this comes down to their job description: they are there to keep the trains running smoothly, not to police the tracks—a job that falls to the railroad police. It's not unheard of for rail employees to radio the dispatcher for information a hobo might be looking for, and will sometimes even let hobos ride with them for a spell, looking for someone to chat with on a long haul.

A more technical approach, and the one favored by "recreational" hobos, is to use a scanner. By tuning to the frequency used by the particular railroad company you're hoping to ride, you'll be able to hear the train dispatchers and engineers relaying information back and forth. Then you'll know which trains are coming in, which are going out, where they're going, and time estimates for each leg.

In the end, a lot of this boils down to doing actual field research in the town or city you're in and connecting with other hobos either in person or over the Internet. By hanging around the yards and doing a little reconnaissance you'll get a pretty good feel for what the travel patterns are. And while this isn't something you'd ask of your grandma or mother-in-law, if you have friends in any of the cities you hope to pass through, you can ask them to scope out the scene for you ahead of time.

Finding the Yards

Before you can hop on a train, you have to find one, and the trains you want to—or should want to—hop on are either completely stopped, or just barely moving. Trains of this type (not moving) are best located in rail yards or just outside of them, before they've gotten up to speed. Providing you're in a city or town and not standing in the middle of a cornfield, you should be able to locate the rail yards. For one thing, freight trains share the same rails as passenger trains, and many places will have signs directing you to either the Amtrak station or, if you're near a major city, the commuter trains. So it becomes a breadcrumb game. Train yards also take up a lot of space and aren't overly attractive, so they tend to be located in large industrial areas. Think warehouses and factories, not suburban developments and shopping malls.

Originally, freight train companies were also responsible for passenger trains, but from 1920 on they did this at an increasing financial loss. In 1970, the government stepped in and created Railpax, intended to continue passenger service but relieving the freight companies of the burden. The name was soon changed to Amtrak (America and track). Amtrak shares the same rail system as the freight trains, and freight trains are required to give Amtrak trains right of way. Which is why the freight train you're riding will pull over when faced with a passenger train.

YARD SAFETY

You need to be really careful when moving around rail yards, and not just because of the bulls. Yards are full of some really heavy machinery—trains among them—that can go into motion without much warning and can severely complicate your life if you happen to be in the process of climbing under or between cars on a train. Particularly at night when stumbling around in the dark, stay alert to your surroundings.

HOPPING THE CAR

Having found the yard and (hopefully) knowing which train you want to take as a result of your impeccable information-gathering endeavors, your next task is to select a car. Don't just hop on to the first car that looks like it will work, but make a note of it. Instead, walk the train looking for the sweetest car. If the train starts to move before you've found it, you can retreat to one of the ones you made a mental note of earlier rather than risk missing the train altogether. One way to know that the train is about to start moving is to listen for the brake test, or brake hiss. This is your signal to find your seat. And forget about the "choo-choo"—that doesn't happen anymore.

flip: To board a moving train.

CARS YOU CAN RIDE

Railroads use several types of cars, but some are definitely better suited to your needs than others—and even among those, some are better than others. Your choice of car may also depend on the weather. Traveling at 70 mph in the winter while exposed to the elements because you climbed on a flat car can suck when it's cold, but wouldn't be half bad in the summer. Boxcars, gondolas, grain cars (often called grainers, or hoppers), piggybacks, doublestacks, car carriers, cabooses, locomotive units, and flat cars are just some of the cars you'll find on the rails. As with anything, there are pros and cons to each.

on the fly: Jumping a moving train. Not a good idea.

As if hopping freight cars wasn't dangerous enough, Jack Dempsey chose one of the even more dangerous methods, known as "riding the rods." On the Pullman railcar, there were two narrow steel rods that ran under the bottom of the car. Hobos would often lodge themselves, lying flat, between the rods and the bottom of the car. A dramatically dangerous way of hopping cars. Manage to fall asleep and roll off and you were done. On a train traveling at full speed, you were never too far away from, as they say, "greasing the tracks."

grease the track: When you're run over by a train, your last act is to lubricate the tracks. "You keep playin' around like that and you're gonna grease the track."

Boxcars

Boxcars are the stereotypical train car with sliding doors on the sides one associates with the hobos of old. Although they used to be the dominant form of rail car, more specialized cars have steadily been replacing them over the years. But you still can find them, and if you find an open one, take it, as traveling in a boxcar offers awesome views while protecting you from the elements and keeping you hidden from the railroad police.

A word of warning: While boxcars seem innocuous, they can pose a serious hazard if you don't heed the following. Once you score a spot on a boxcar, you need to "spike" the door, which means you have to force a railroad spike (you'll have to find one)—or anything else you can find—at the bottom of the door to keep it from closing. If the doors close on you while you're inside—which can happen right when leaving a train yard from slack action—you can pretty much forget about opening them, and you could spend a long time inside, possibly longer than your energy bars and water will hold out. More than a few rail workers have opened up boxcars only to find a dead hobo inside.

Boxcars used by the French in World War II were known as "forty and eights," meaning they could each hold forty soldiers and eight horses. American troops fighting in France found it a less than desirable form of travel, and later, to commemorate their shared experience, an American veterans group named their organization the "Forty and Eight."

Gondolas

A gondola car is an open car with walls, somewhat like a container car if you removed the upper half. These are great to ride when they're empty. Not so much when loaded: You can be on one side of the car daydreaming about what your friends would say if they could see you now while the load sits on the other, and one abrupt stop-and-go movement later there's a manufacturer at the end of the line wondering why his rebar came with a hobo head attached to it.

Hoppers/Grainers

Hopper cars are similar to gondola cars, but the bottom slopes down to the middle from each end, which funnels the cargo—coal, fertilizer, grain, etc., down toward hinged doors that open to enable the cargo to unload through gravity. There are both covered and uncovered hopper cars. They are often called grain cars, or grainers, after a common load they carried.

What these have going for them are not just the "porches" at either end, which make for perfect roosts, but by squeezing yourself through a hole at either end, you'll find a small space where you can really lay back. Just be warned: it's a real buzz kill should you board an open hopper in motion, hike yourself over the side, and slide down to discover an open door leading directly to the tracks below. Then you're like a carrot being fed into a food processor. Or something to that effect.

Piggybacks

Piggyback cars are tractor trailers (minus the cab) getting a piggyback ride on a flat train car. You can hop up on one of these, and hang between the wheels of the trailer.

Double-Stacks

Double-stack cars are shipping containers stacked one on top of the other, both of them riding on a well car (basically a flat car with low sides hugging the bottom container). Freight companies love the method, as it can double the amount of freight a train can carry, and you can love them because of the wells you can ride in at the front and back of the car.

Autoracks

Autoracks, or car carriers, were developed to carry cars. Initially the railroads just transported automobiles single file on flat bed cars, but soon realized it was a pretty inefficient use of space and that they could double, and then even triple, the number of cars by adding levels above the first row. Hobos of the modern age who happened upon autoracks had struck gold. With the cars they carried often unlocked and with the key inside, you could travel across the country with your leather seat reclined and the heat on while blasting Lynyrd Skynyrd. If that's what you wanted. Increasingly, however, autoracks are of the enclosed variety, and while getting in is not impossible, it's not so easy, either.

> In the seventies, GM came out with the Chevrolet Vega, a compact car. In conjunction with Southern Pacific, they created a specialized new rail car, the Vert-A-Pac, which was designed to hold rows of Vegas vertically, somewhat akin to the racks in front of racks at the dry cleaners. Had the Vega been a huge success, it might have offset the costs of having to fabricate reinforced frame members on the car's underside that could hold on to the racks without the car coming apart. But the Vega was not a huge seller, and neither was the Vert-A-Pac.

Cabooses

Unfortunately, you'll have to drop any romantic notions of riding on the little red caboose at the end of a train. For one, they're disappearing, and the ones that *are* still around are almost never red. Originally cabooses held up the rear of the train so crew members could operate track switches and keep an eye on the back cars. They also served as the crew's quarters. But as technology advanced—primarily with the introduction of an automated system nicknamed FRED—the caboose lost its pivotal role, and by the 1960s was becoming merely the stuff of children's books. You can still find them on smaller local lines where it's more cost-effective to hire switchmen than implement a new system, and you can also find them in many rail yards sitting by themselves and mostly forgotten (which when accessible, are great places to camp out).

> Cabooses have largely been replaced by FREDs, an acronym for "flashing rear-end device." Attached to the back of the last car of a train, the FRED monitors air-brake pressure and train movement and relays the information to the engineer up front, something previously done by a crew member in a caboose.

Flat Cars

Flat cars are just that. A tundra on wheels. Riding these gives no protection from the weather, you're completely visible, and with no raised sides the chances of getting bounced right off by shifting cargo can outweigh the benefits of getting on.

GETTING ON THAT CAR

Hopping a moving freight car can require your best Mary Lou Retton, and she wasn't hefting around a fifty-pound pack. Given that you're not her, and you are carrying that pack, you should keep the idea somewhere just above putting your hand down a garbage disposal. But of course, sometimes you have to put your hand down the garbage disposal, so if you do try and mount a moving train, it's best if you're with someone who has done it a few times before who can show you the ropes. Make sure you've walked a train or two and really studied the different kinds of cars and what you can hold on to. What you don't want to do is find a train in motion and building up speed, and then blindly pick a car and hop on. You might discover you're on a car with no place to safely sit, and at this point the train may not just be going too fast for you to jump off, but also may not stop for another ten or twelve hours. If you study up on the car types and what they look like and where to grab on, you can avoid this.

You have to be running with the train and not against it, and you want, as closely as you can, to be moving at the same speed as the train to make a smooth transition; if the train cars are flying past you, it's not gonna happen. So, assuming that your train is moving and that you're moving alongside and matching its speed, you have two options: one, you throw your pack in first and then try to board—the benefit being that you can perform the necessary physical trickery unencumbered and the drawback being that should you proceed to fail to get on the train, you just lost your luggage; or two, you try boarding the train with your pack on your back. You won't lose your bag this way, but while you are trying to direct your momentum in one direction your pack will be holding you back. In choosing between the two, tossing your pack in first is preferable. Better to lose your goods than your legs.

TEN EYE-POPPING RIDES

The *Hobo Times* compiled a list of the top ten scenic rides in the United States.

1. Take the Lamoille Valley and Maine Central between Sheldon Junction, Vermont, and Portland, Maine. This will take you through both the Green and White Mountains in New England. Noted for being best in the fall.
2. Ride the Norfolk and Western between Hagerstown, Maryland, and Knoxville, Tennessee. See the Shenandoah Valley,

Blue Ridge Mountains, the Appalachian Mountains, and Great Smokey Mountains National Park.

3. Between Jacksonville and Miami, ride the Florida East Coast Railroad. A 350-mile coastal ride of palm, coconut, and fruit trees.
4. Follow alongside the Mississippi River on the Burlington Northern between Fort Madison, Iowa, and Memphis, Tennessee.
5. Take the Denver and Rio Grande Western alongside the Arkansas River with the Rocky Mountains in the background between Pueblo, Colorado, and Glenwood Springs, Colorado.
6. Between Cheyenne, Wyoming, and Laurel, Montana, ride the Burlington Northern and check out the Big Horn Mountains and River, all the while passing through what still looks like the Wild West.
7. See Glacier National Park, Whitefish, and head up the Continental Divide on the Burlington Northern, this time between Spokane, Washington, and Cut Bank, Montana.
8. From Sacramento, California, to Klamath Falls, Oregon, start out crossing the American river, follow Feather River Canyon, and then head through the Sierras on the Union Pacific.
9. Between Colton, California, and Salt Lake City, Utah, take the Union Pacific. Spectacular views in the mountains and desert valleys filled with flowers in the spring.
10. Ride along 100 miles of deserted beaches and the Pacific Ocean between Oxnard and San Luis Obispo, California, on the Southern Pacific.

Safety on the Train

There are several things to be aware of while riding a freight train. They tell you to keep your arms and hands inside the car when you're riding a roller coaster, and the same goes for riding on a train. Maybe due to some strange holdover from being three years old, it can be flat out irresistible to sit down on a car and dangle your legs over the edge. But traveling at 75 mph with any number of objects placed along railroad tracks, all it takes is one bad bump to separate you from your legs, and the same thing can result if a boxcar door slides shut while you're sitting like that.

> Kenneth Howe, in his article "American Nomads" for *SFGate*, relates a ride in a boxcar he took with North Bank Fred, a veteran recreational hopper. Shortly after they were well under way, North Bank was hollering something at him, and after he took his earplugs out he heard him yelling that the door was closing. And it was, the original six-foot opening was down to three and as the train ground to a halt, it had shrunk again—leaving an opening of just a foot and a half. Be prepared for some serious noise. This is a great time to bust out the earplugs that you so cleverly brought with you. The auditory attack can be bad, but only a nuisance when compared to some of the physical dangers. Train cars have slack between them, and "slack action" refers to the massive jolt that can occur when a train starts to move and the slack is suddenly taken up. If you're sitting there with your head against a wall, the experience can be the equivalent to someone slamming the back of your head into the pavement.

Hump yards are specialized yards where a small hill—or hump—leads down to several tracks. At the top, cars are pushed over and directed to one of the tracks to eventually form shipments all heading in the same direction. Many freight train companies advertise their hump yards as "gentle," but what you would consider gentle is probably altogether different. Just another time where you can get really rattled when you least expect it.

OTHER METHODS OF TRANSPORT

There are often times when traveling by freight train isn't feasible for a variety of reasons. You may be in a place without a yard where the trains pass at 60 mph and never stop, or maybe you just want a roaming lifestyle without risking life and limb hopping freight trains. The hobos of the early twentieth century rode freight trains because their only other viable options were to walk or steal a horse. You can still choose these options, but the path of least resistance may be to bike, hitchhike, take a bus or passenger train, or carpool with someone headed in your direction (or you could decide wherever they're going is your direction).

Bike

They say riding by freight train is a way to travel by going through the country's backyards, and another form of travel more intimate than car or bus is to travel by bike. While it's illegal to take your bike on the interstate (and why would you want to?), pretty much every other road is fair game. In addition, the U.S. Bicycle Route System is an expanding network of official routes throughout the United States, linking cities composed of both shared roadways and trails.

As opposed to the other forms of travel, this will take a certain degree of physical fitness—which if you don't have starting out, you will shortly.

They do make trailers you can haul by bike, but panniers (the bags attaching to either side of both the front and rear wheels) can be a more flexible option, particularly when you might be needing to carry your bike through a bit or rough terrain while camping—also a reason to travel with the lightest bike you can find or afford.

Make sure you travel with a complete set of bike tools, lights, and reflectors, and if you're new to biking, get well acquainted with your bike and its maintenance before heading out. Not the kind of stuff you want to be figuring out stranded in the middle of nowhere at night.

Hitchhiking

As opposed to train hopping, where you risk announcing your presence to the authorities mostly in train yards, if you hitchhike, you are right out there for everyone to see. But contrary to popular belief, hitchhiking is not illegal in every state, although it can still be tricky and is often an issue of semantics.

In states where they've tried to make it illegal, but don't come right out and *call* it illegal, the basic wording is as follows: "No person shall stand in a roadway for the purpose of soliciting a ride." Some states throw in "soliciting a ride from a driver," but it's pretty much all the same. That may seem fairly cut and dry: You can't be on the road looking for a ride. But here's the rub: the definition of roadway, in almost all of these laws, specifically excludes the shoulder. In other words, you can't stand in the middle of the road with your thumb in the air, but if you're standing along it, you're good. Of course, explaining this to an officer is an entirely different story altogether and you may end up with a ticket just for being a smartass.

Hitchhiking can be like going on a blind date—you have no idea what you're getting yourself into. Your driver could be a great and interesting person, a person who can't stop talking about the precise subjects you have absolutely zero interest in, or a creepy and somewhat fear-inducing person you wish you'd let pass by.

The Bus

This is pretty self-explanatory. Find the bus station, pick a place, buy a ticket, and get a ride that will almost always include a restroom, heat, and air conditioning, and maybe even some TV. Similar to hitchhiking, you may also have to sit next to somebody who feels his life is just too important not to share, and this can make for a long ride. But life is give and take, so be it.

doggin' it: To ride by bus, particularly a Greyhound.

Ride with a Ticket

Then, of course, there's the mode of travel that may seem against what every hobo stands for: Amtrak. But it works; it's a train, and sometimes you won't have a choice. Occasionally when scouting for a freight car to catch, railroad police may approach (after all, they're trained to be suspicious of folks roaming the railroad tracks with big packs). If there's an Amtrak station nearby, you might say, "I'm waiting for an Amtrak train but wanted to check out the tracks." They might like the story, but only agree to leave your side when you actually enter the station. Grin and bear it. Other advantages to passenger train travel: It can be really comfortable, is 100 percent legal, runs on a schedule, has a bathroom and a food car, and most conveniently, you don't have to be able to pole vault to get on board.

Carpooling

Carpooling is a little like hitchhiking except (for the most part) you don't arrange it while standing on the side of the road. If hitchhiking is a little like cold calling people, finding a carpool is more like following up on leads. You can find people looking for someone to travel with in almost any place. Check out local bulletin boards in small grocery stores or coffee shops. But expect to find the real jackpot online. There are an endless number of places to find rides. Look on Craigslist, Digihitch, or Squat the Planet. You may not have a car, but someone else may have one but no means to run it (money for gas). In that way, it can be a symbiotic relationship. There are always people out there looking for a traveling buddy or for someone to split costs. You can either find someone looking, or you can post that you're looking for a ride. Odds are good that you'll link up with someone.

TRAVELING SAFE

While traveling solo has its benefits, it's never a bad idea to travel with someone else—in addition to warding off loneliness, you never know what kind of situation might come up in which having a wingman could help. For one thing, it's a whole lot easier if you need to make a run into a store or across the street for a few minutes if you can leave your pack with someone trustworthy to watch it while you're doing your quick errand. Additionally, if you have a camp set up and aren't ready to completely pack up but just need to head into town for some supplies, again, it's great to have someone who can stay behind and keep an eye on things.

Traveling with another is also great for safety. Lone travelers can be easy targets, whereas two people will almost always give someone pause (especially if they're thinking of causing chaos). This is particularly true of the railroads these days. There are a lot of people riding the rails other than hobos, and you can't assume everyone's friendly. Remember: In choosing to live life off the beaten path, you've also given up a lot of the protection that comes with living within society's boundaries.

In addition, with a travel buddy you'll have someone you can lean on when you sprain your ankle hopping off a train, someone to grab your hand and pull you up in dramatic fashion while you dangle out the door of a boxcar, and someone to carry the tent and cookstove for a bit when you're ready to just drop like a parched wanderer in the desert. You'll also be able to double your resources: You might know someone you could stay with just outside of Chicago, your buddy might have some family in Colorado with some room to spare, and he also might have that missing key ingredient that can change dinner into something worth remembering.

It's especially smart for female travelers to travel with someone else. Although uncommon, women travelers have been known to run into trouble, and having a travel partner can increase your safety. Regardless of sex, you'll want to be especially attuned to your surroundings at all times, and if you're about to hop a freight train and there's someone else already in the car, consider finding another. It's mostly commonsense stuff, but remember, you're more vulnerable when traveling alone.

Sylvia Siebken, a Depression-era hobo, never wanted people to be aware that she and her traveling companion were women. So they did what a lot of female hobos did in those days: They wore "bib overalls," tucked their hair up under their hats, and essentially, dressed like men.

FOLKS TO WATCH OUT FOR

In addition to just being wary of other travelers you'll come across, there are a few more specific categories of folks to look out for; namely bulls and members of the FTRA (Freight Train Riders of America). Your risk of physical danger from the bulls working today is nothing compared to what it was like in years past; most of the trouble you'll get from them is of the legal variety. But from the FTRA, there is a larger risk to your person and property.

The Bulls

Who and what are these infamous "bulls" hobos are always referring to? They are railroad police, and their job has always been to keep people who aren't supposed to be on trains off of trains. Historically, they were known for having the capacity to be pretty rough. Many a hobo received a good working over by a bull, and there are plenty of stories of bulls coming across hobos on trains and making them jump while the train was at full tilt. Occasionally they would even take pot shots at them from the train.

Today their job remains pretty much the same, though today their goal is to keep trains and yards free of trespassers for legal reasons—people get hurt, and freight companies don't want to be held liable. You'll find railroad police in rail yards, usually in a vehicle, so if you stay off the roads, you have a good chance at eluding them. If you are on a train and waiting for it to go, the sound of stone under foot is a telltale sign a bull is near. Of course, it could just be another hobo like yourself, or just someone unfriendly. In any case, it behooves you to steer clear of bulls.

If you get caught these days, you're not going to end up in a labor camp or on a chain gang—you'll most likely just be kicked out of the yard or given a ticket, but depending on the bull, a short stay in jail is not completely out of the question. If issued a ticket, you'll have to appear in court, and if you skip that part, you'll also want to skip coming back to the town for a long time.

> "It rarely pays to stop and enter into explanations with bulls when they look 'horstile.' A swift get-away is the thing to do. It took me some time to learn this; but the finishing touch was put upon me by a bull in New York City. Ever since that time it has been an automatic process with me to make a run for it when I see a bull reaching for me. This automatic process has become a mainspring of conduct in me, wound up and ready for instant release. I shall never get over it. Should I be eighty years old, hobbling along the street on crutches, and should a policeman suddenly reach out for me, I know I'd drop the crutches and run like a deer."
>
> —Jack London, describing his take on bulls, in *The Road*.

Freight Train Riders of America

The Freight Train Riders of America, or the FTRA, has become somewhat legendary, and as the conventional wisdom goes, if you're not one of them, you don't want to run into them. They started up in the 1980s as a group of train riders looking to form a community (supposedly their name started out as F★★★ The Reagan Administration), and as a group, they have been suspected of having a fairly heavy criminal component. They mostly ride the BNSF in the Northwest, where you may recognize them by the black bandanas they are known to wear around their necks, clasped with silver rings. There are two smaller groups, as well, who primarily ride the CSX. Those on the lines in the South identify themselves with red bandanas and silver rings, and those coming through the

Midwest will wear blue bandanas with silver rings. Still, despite all the ballyhoo and midnight ghost stories, there are many hobos who have encountered them with no problem.

> ⚠ **REMEMBER:** You don't mix well with steel, and hopping a freight train is no simple business. There are a variety of other ways to travel, and while safety may seem boring, bored is better than dead. Throughout your journey, stay vigilant, and keep your personal safety a top priority.

Did You Know Boxer Jack Dempsey Hoboed?

Jack Dempsey (originally William Harrison Dempsey, after the president) was born in Manassa, Colorado, in 1895. While he would later become infamous as the Manassa Mauler, boxing's heavyweight champion of the world from 1919 to 1927, he's a little less known for the years he spent hopping freight trains from town to town, fighting in saloons, and sometimes in barns, as Kid Blackie.

One of eleven children (or even thirteen by some accounts) his family was poor and moved around a lot; his father and his brothers were miners, and they would move through Colorado and Utah while following the mining work. By the time he was eight, William was already doing work on a nearby farm and, dropping out of school after eighth grade, he went on to pick up odd jobs shining shoes and crop picking, and unloading beets at a sugar refinery for ten cents a ton.

One of his older brothers, Bernie, was also a boxer, and picked up extra money by fighting in the mining towns. He started teaching William the basics, which, in addition to how to throw a punch, included soaking his face in brine to strengthen the skin and keep it from splitting easily, and chewing pine tar gum to keep his jaw strong.

He left home in 1911 to work in the mines, and as the story goes, while working alongside his brother in Utah, one of the other miners started taunting him. He took it for a while, but when he finally got fed up, he started prancing around the guy ready for some fisticuffs. Amused, a crowd gathered and bets were placed. In moves the whole world would soon come to know, with one punch, the kid knocked the guy out with a right to the jaw.

Soon he was entering saloons and announcing, "I can't sing. I can't dance. But I'll lick anyone in the house." He's also said to have gone up to bartenders and asked them to pick out a guy they'd like to see get put down. Sixteen years old and only 130 pounds, he initially found plenty of takers. But after brutally taking guys out, word spread fast, and he'd have to go to another town to fight, as no one else cared to take him on.

Although some debate whether to call him an actual hobo, from 1911 to 1916, Dempsey traveled from town to town, riding the rods through Colorado, Utah, and Nevada, picking up whatever work he could—he washed floors, picked fruit, chopped trees, and even worked as a laborer for the circus. But whenever he got the chance, he would fight for his food and money.

Jim Murray, a sportswriter, in later years commented, "Whenever I hear the name, Jack Dempsey, I think of an America that was one big roaring camp of miners, drifters, bunkhouse hands, con men, hard cases, men who lived by their fists and their shooting irons and by the cards they drew. America at high noon."

CHAPTER 4

Getting Settled

FINDING A BED FOR THE NIGHT AND, IDEALLY, A MEAL

"If we had some eggs we could have ham and eggs, if we had some ham."

—GROUCHO MARX

Sleeping and eating will no longer be passive activities for you, but instead the hard-won results of your ingenuity. In this chapter we'll look at different ways to accomplish each; some you'll undoubtedly find a little more palatable than others. If you're not planning on staying in an existing jungle or making your own camp but are instead looking for a couch—or even just a backyard or porch—to crash on, you have some resources a hobo during the depression would have thought nothing of short of space travel.

VIRTUAL COUCHES

A fairly new method available to you for obtaining a place to sleep is through online travel groups. Several websites, such as couchsurfing.org and CouchSwap, are actually dedicated to this. Within minutes you can be connected with people all over the United States offering their extra (or, at least you'll hope it's "extra") space for a night or two. This is also where your networking skills come in to play. You're going to meet a lot of people, and by talking and sharing, you'll be surprised at the opportunities that might present themselves. If you're an ornery recluse full of snide comments and general unpleasantness, you may find yourself spending more time than others sleeping in ditches.

> Everyone ends up in a ditch at some point. Kerouac recounts having hopped a freight train at night outside of L.A. and realizing too late, after the train was picking up speed, that it was entirely made up of sealed cars with no access. He was forced to jump, and spent the rest of the night in a ditch by the tracks.

COMMUNAL LIVING

Don't overlook the local hostel. These are generally cheap and geared for function over form, although fancier ones do exist; in which case, you could find your own room at a motel for just a few bucks more. But keep in mind that hostels are good places to meet other travelers, maybe find a traveling buddy, or just learn of good opportunities further down the road.

THE OLD-TIMEY WAY

You could always attempt the traditional method of trying to obtain lodging in exchange for work. Most likely this won't work out so well in cities, where no one makes eye contact and everyone's wary of meeting the next serial killer. Bumping into someone at a coffee shop with three minutes to spare doesn't give you enough time to make a good case that you deserve a couch for the night. But in rural areas where people have barns and people aren't in such a rush to be somewhere, your chances of making real contact with good people who are willing to give you the benefit of the doubt can be pretty good. People with houses almost always have something that needs doing, and a person willing to do anything from cleaning out a basement to planting tomato seeds can prove he's trustworthy and earn a place to sleep.

THE CONCRETE JUNGLE

So you just hopped off a train and you're wondering "what next?" Depending on the hour and whether you're in a rural or urban area, it's either time to head in to town and see what's up or it's time to set up your camp. If you were anticipating a city, hopefully you've planned ahead and already made arrangements for the night, either by knowing the location of a hostel or a cheap hotel or you're staying with friends, family, or folks you've found online.

If there's a twenty-four-hour bus or passenger train station nearby, you can spend the night there—provided you don't look like you're squatting, or you may end up getting hassled by the police. But if you just act like another traveler who has to wait around for their connecting train or bus, you should be OK. If you're looking a bit dirty around the edges, make use of the public restroom to clean up, as disheveled people hanging around public transportation stations end up attracting more unwanted attention. You can also seek out a shelter (which are often full by evening—if this is what you're looking for get there early), but just setting up shop in an alley, on a doorstep, or under a bridge may be asking for trouble. Clearly, the more well-to-do an area seems, the safer it will likely be. Assess the situation and use common sense. And don't forget graveyards—they can be perfect.

boil up: To get cleaned up. Originated from the practice of boiling clothes to kill off lice.

IN THE BUSH

If you end up alongside the tracks in a rural setting with some woods around, you'll need to set up your own jungle. After sitting on a big boulder for a few minutes, the full realization that you've left it all behind may hit you upside the back of the head and make you see things differently. For starters, you may start to understand that besides what's required for self-preservation in a natural environment, there is actually nothing you actually need to do. You could twiddle your thumbs for an hour and no one will tell you to get back to work. Nor will anyone tell you to move your car because today is street cleaning, or tell you to tuck in your shirt because "today is really important," or say "thank you for your interest but unfortunately there were other, more qualified, applicants." You are your own island. If you've got food with you, some knowledge of how to get by in the wild (or at least your wits about you), and a good set of gear, there's no rush. Don't feel like working tomorrow? Don't. Feel like taking a nap? Do it. There's no checkout time, and the only thing you'll need to get out of this place is a passing train.

The Ideal Location

Venture in a bit to avoid detection. If you're just staying for a night you don't need to stress too much on where you put yourself, but if you've managed to pull in a job in a nearby town or just plan on staying in one place for an extended period, you'll want to give careful consideration to where you set up camp. Familiarize yourself with your surroundings. No point in getting up in the middle of the night to pee and falling into a gulley you could have avoided had you looked around beforehand. And don't forget to take a look up. Any large dead limbs directly above? If so, set up your sleeping arrangements elsewhere. They can fall with little warning and are way worse than an alarm clock.

Gullies. Don't set up camp in one. Gullies look like gullies because they've been shaped by running water, and while it may look dry now, it can look a whole lot different in a flash flood. Should this happen, you could drown, or at the very least lose some of your gear and find the rest scattered and many of your supplies ruined.

"Lodging" and the Seasons

The prime spot for you depends on weather conditions and the season. In summer, you need to worry about avoiding bugs, your proximity to water, and getting ample protection from rain and sun. Try to choose a site that's near a moving stream or on top of a ridge so that the breezes will keep the bugs at bay. In winter, you need to worry about finding shelter from wind and precipitation and a dry place for a fire and sleeping nook. Choose a sheltered area to set up your camp. You will also want to consider whether or not you want people to be able to see your camp. You probably don't. Boughs of trees can be used as camouflage screens to prevent your camp from being discovered by the heavies, potential ruffians, and just the yeggs in general. If there's snow, you can also build a snow mound which would provide shelter, but make for some pretty chilly hands if you didn't bring gloves along.

yegg: A traveling thief.

Digging In

For a semipermanent camp, a lean-to is an easy and effective structure that will keep you dry and out of the wind and make for great pictures to share with your grandchildren. First, note the direction of the prevailing winds (you can finally lick your finger and stick it in the air like you know what you're doing). You'll want the rear of your structure facing the wind, leaving the open side protected. Next, try and find two trees at least eight feet apart that can serve as the support for the structure. Find a long, sturdy stick and tie it running between the two trees, at a height a little above your head. Locate several other sturdy sticks, and lean them up against the support beam running between the two trees. If you brought a tarp, tie it across the leaning sticks, forming a waterproof barrier. If it's just you, make sure that the area under the tarp is at least large enough to allow for a dry area for sleeping.

THE ALL-IMPORTANT FIRE PIT

For a multipurpose fire that serves as both a heat source and a cooking area, build a fire pit. First, pick a place. Look for an area of dry soil where you can dig a shallow hole in the ground. Next, ring your pit with large stones, but avoid using such porous rocks as shale or river rocks (these can hold water and when they get hot can actually explode and send rock shrapnel in every direction). If you can find it, granite is your best bet. Finally, if the ground is wet or snow-covered, make a platform of logs, stones, or sticks on which you will build your fire to keep it dry and burning.

> Your goal is not to start a forest fire. That's the opposite of low-key and creates big problems for everybody, plus, when you get back home and your friends say, "Man, did you hear about that forest fire?" you don't want to have to sheepishly say, "Yeah, that was me." No fun. Make sure there are no overhanging branches above your pit that could catch fire. The danger zone shifts with the wind. Keep this in mind as you set up your camp.

To start the fire, gather tinder that will catch easily. You can use dry twigs, bark, wood shavings, paper, dry grass, or dried animal dung (but steer clear of poison ivy or poison oak). Birch bark and pine branches are especially flammable, so if you have access to them, use 'em. Make a small pile of the tinder, and build a pyramid of larger sticks above it. Light the tinder with a match or a lighter, and once the larger sticks have started burning you can add a log or two. Consider packing waterproof matches—they'll help you out when conditions are on the soggy side.

You probably grew up being told never to leave the iron on. Now you have to remember never to leave your camp with the fire on. Really. Don't take a quick look at it and think, "Yup, looks out," and continue on your merry way. Make sure your fire is out, completely, before you leave; it can't be stressed enough. Most likely you're not going to have enough water to thoroughly douse it, so add in dirt and stir it around well enough until the coals are cold. Burying the fire is not sufficient, as it can still burn away under there and eventually ignite something. And never go to sleep with the fire still going. You're just asking for trouble nobody wants.

The All-Important Bear Bag (If You're in an Area with Bears, That Is)

If you're camping in the northern and central plains you can probably get along without this—which is good. There aren't a whole lot of trees there to hang one from anyway.

Bears love food, and have some incredible sniffers; it's said their sense of smell is seven times that of a bloodhound, and the last thing you want is a bear tearing through your tent in the middle of the night because you left a candy bar wrapper in your bag. Bear bags are the solution.

Look for a tree whose limb extends away from the trunk (which, conveniently, most do). A good limb allows you to hang your food bag a minimum of four feet from the trunk and more than ten feet from the ground. The size of the limb is important, because you want one that's strong enough to support the weight of your grub bag but not nearly strong enough to support the weight of a bear. You will also need a strong bag to hold your food, and about forty feet of rope.

There are several ways to hang a bag, and while the easiest isn't the most effective, it is the easiest. Tie one end of the rope to your food bag and the other end around a rock with some heft to it that can counter the weight of your bag. Throw the rock over the limb (might take a few shots), the weight of the rock will pull the rope down on the other side so that you can reach it. Then hoist your bear bag up at least ten feet and tie the free end off around a nearby tree.

I'M HUNGRY; WHERE'S THE FOOD?

So you leave for the road and you've got your pack filled with water, six packs of dehydrated instant dinner, and a few energy bars. And then the food runs out, as it will do when you eat it, and now you don't have any food anymore.

You are now a hunter/gatherer. Gone are the days when at the first pang of hunger you just needed to make a short trek to the fridge, and when you opened the doors you were confronted by a world of endless wonders. It may not have seemed like it then, but it does now that you're out on the trail with nothing left in your pack. Your circumstances have changed.

Finding Food

Sure, you can procure all of your snacks and supplies from a 7-Eleven, but you're out here to be self sufficient, and after risking life and limb to get here, what toughened hobo wants to rely on societal training wheels and ask the clerk if they have a microwave to heat up the frozen taquitos?

You have a lot of options when it comes to grub. For starters, here's a list of some great staple foods to consider packing or buying along the way. Some can be an entire meal by themselves and others are more to be used as supplements. And clearly, some heavy foodstuffs (like potatoes) you don't want to be hauling around for too long, but if you're staying put for a bit they can work. Same goes for eggs. You probably won't be eating a lot of them unless the great outdoors has become a giant refrigerator and you are especially good at packing delicate items, but there are plenty of other options for food that pack and travel quite well:

* Rice
* Quinoa
* Lentils
* Split Peas
* Citrus Fruits
* Apples/Pears
* Carrots
* Potatoes
* Sweet Potatoes
* Garlic
* Flour
* Salt
* Powdered Milk
* Nuts
* Dried Fruit
* Cooking Oil

Fishing

If there's a lake or river nearby, you could have an endless supply of fish. When you head out on your expedition, remember that fish may not be brilliant, but they're not dummies, either. They will hang out in the most comfortable spot depending on the day. This means that on a hot summer day you should look in a deep shady pool, whereas on a chilly day you will find them in a sunny, shallow area. In general, they like the shelter of an overhang or a submerged rock or log.

Fishing kits are small and lightweight, generally consisting of just a line, some hooks, lures, weights, and floats. You can carry a fishing rod with you, or you can improvise on the spot with a long stick. Chances are you'll feel a little more badass when you manage to bag a few lake trout with nothing more than a hook, line, and a random stick.

If you don't have any hooks, but you do have some line, you can reach back into your primal self and bring back an old trick: the gorge.

MAKING YOUR GORGE

1. Find a piece of hard wood, or even a piece of deer bone.
2. Use your knife to whittle it down until it's about 1½ to 2 inches long and sharp at both ends.
3. In the center, make a small groove that you'll tie the fishing line around.
4. Now, attach some bait or a lure on it.

Basic idea is to cast it into the water, the fish will see your Trojan horse but not know it's one and swallow the pointy contraption, and as soon as you feel a tug on the other end of the line, give it a good yank and you'll have lodged the gorge in the fish's gullet. Haul 'er in.

Catching a fish brings on the instant feeling of success . . . usually followed by a slight panic. Now what? Grab him, squeeze his mouth open to see the manner in which he's hooked, and then reverse the hook's direction to pull it out. The fish is not going to just take this abuse, but will actively be working against you. Keep a firm grip.

If you have no hooks *and* no line, but you are still dying for a good fish fry, you can try your skill at spearing. Sharpen a stick with one or more points, wade into the water, and wait with your spear tip as close to the water as possible until you see your target. When you're feeling the moment, strike out and pin the fish to the bottom.

If you have fished in the past and are used to throwing it back in, resist the urge—it's time to learn a new skill. First option is to grab it by the tail and swing it into something hard, the goal being to break its neck (or what would be its neck if it had one). Chances are the first attempt will do little more than make it mad. Do it again, and again, if you have to. Suddenly, fishing may seem like more of a contact sport than just sitting on a rock meditating while you become one with the natural world around you.

Second option is to hit the fish behind the head with a hard object. You could use a pot if you've got nothing else, which you probably don't. Fish whackers wasn't on your supplies list. But be good to the fish—don't wimp out and leave him to die a slow death by suffocation.

HOW TO GUT A FISH

You've got the fish, knocked it unconscious, and now you're staring at the thing and wondering where to start. You know the next thing you have to do is clean and gut it, but if you weren't in the Scouts or didn't have an avid fishing fan in the family, you might be feeling a little daunted. It all seems pretty simple when it's sitting on your plate and looking like anything but something that was just swimming around in the water, but getting it to your plate . . .

Hold that fish flat, and take your knife and insert it at the base of the jaw and cut through the chest bone all the way down the length of the fish until you reach the end. If you can, try not to stick the knife too far in or you'll puncture the innards and have more of a mess on your hands than you've already got. At this point, things are probably getting a bit smelly.

With the fish split, reach your fingers in and pull out the guts from the top to the bottom. The liver will be attached to the backbone of the fish, and you'll need to cut that out separately. With everything out, unless you plan on eating it, this is a good time to cut off the head, doing so from behind the gills. You don't have to scale the fish to cook and eat it, though don't try eating the skin if you haven't scaled it—they won't kill you, but in general, fish scales taste pretty damn awful.

To scale it, use any tool at your disposal that's flat and thin and scrape from the tail toward the head. If you're applying enough pressure, scales should be flying all over the place. Get them all off, paying special attention to the back of the head where it can be easy to miss. Cut the fins off as well.

Given your lack of refrigeration, if it's summer, plan on cooking and eating your fish fairly quickly. It won't last long. In winter, however, if there's snow, first gut the fish and then you can pack it in the snow. As long as it stays cold, the fish should be okay for a few days.

Foraging for Plants and Berries

If you run out of food out there and think you'll survive by eating plants and berries, think again. Unless you *really* know what you're doing, you're likely to ingest something that will feel a whole lot worse than being hungry and could leave you quite dead after a slow and painful ordeal filled with lots of throwing up and dry heaves and acute pain in the gut along with a lot of sweating. Another thing to consider is that the energy it takes for you to go foraging for things you're not even sure of will most likely outweigh any energy you might gain from eating the few leaves or berries you're actually able to discover.

Christopher McCandless, on whom the book *Into the Wild* is based, is thought to have survived more than 110 days in the Alaskan interior by foraging for his own food. They think he confused two plants that look almost identical, and unfortunately ate the wrong one, which led to his inability to digest other food. Eventually this made him too weak to leave the bus that was his shelter, and he died of starvation.

WARNING: There are plenty of poisonous plants out there. In order to avoid getting sick, you must have a good foraging guidebook with clear pictures. Generally, drawings are easier to interpret than photographs. Also, be aware that some plants are endangered and should not be harmed. Try to obtain information on the endangered status of plants in the states where you are foraging. Think like a conservationist, only take the parts that you need, and leave the rest to grow and thrive and provide food for others.

As a rule of thumb, ferns and grasses are not edible. But clearly, some things are fine. Blackberries and blueberries are pretty easy to identify and make for some tasty treats while hiking. Here are some reliable and easily identifiable picks:

* Acorns. These nutritious staples are quite bitter when improperly prepared because they have a very high tannin content. To get rid of the tannins, peel the nuts and boil them in successive changes of water until the water is clear and colorless. The acorns can then be eaten or dried, and even powdered for later use.
* Dandelions. Use the leaves as salad greens. They are best in the spring and fall.
* Cattails. These can be found in every state. Look for wet areas. The white shoots are delicious steamed like asparagus. In early summer the green male flowers can be cooked and eaten like corn, although they tend to be a bit dry. The pollen can be collected in mid-summer and kept as a nutritious addition to dishes. In winter, the roots can be dug from the cold muck and mashed, dried, and pounded to collect their starch to thicken soups.
* Ramps. Similar to leeks, you'll find these in the mountains of the South. Wild onions make everything wilder. Or, at least they do when the only other thing you have to eat is some white rice and a day old bagel.
* Berries. Raspberries, blackberries, strawberries, thimble berries, mulberries, the list is long and delicious. Since the berry season is short and sweet, these can be dried to store for later use.
* Amaranth. The leaves are edible cooked or raw, but the real value is in the seeds. To collect the seeds, cut the flower heads in the late summer or fall and let them dry. Once dried, you can

rub or shake the grains free from the flowers. This grain is super nutritious and stores easily.

* Fennel. Celery meets licorice. The stalks can be used to make a plank for roasting fish, or as a stuffing in a roasted bird. The young leaves can be used as flavoring additions in any dish. The pollen and seeds store well and can be used to add flavor and nutrition to food.
* Nettles. The leaves and young shoots are nutritious, tasty, and boost the immune system. But be careful when harvesting them! Gloves will protect you from the sting. Boil them in two changes of water to completely remove the sting before eating.
* Kudzu. The tender spring shoots can be cooked like spinach and the roots can be collected for their starch, much like cattail roots. Grows like weeds in the South.
* Pawpaws. These are a true American delicacy. They can be found throughout the states east of the great plains. When ripe, the fruit will be soft like a peach.
* Purslane. You'll love it. Can steam it, cook it, put it in soups, or add fresh to your salads.

Dumpster Diving

When you're not in the wild-wild, but find yourself in urban or suburban parts, this can be a viable option. Whether it's referred to as dumpster diving, going freegan, eating at D-Mart, binning, tatting, urban foraging, or simply finding your dinner in a garbage can, digging through the trash can solve the very serious problem of being really hungry without a cent in your pocket. It can also be tremendously rewarding—or some seriously unpleasant business—depending on the dumpster you raid.

The closest you may have come to this in the past is being seated in a restaurant, the food or service is taking forever, and you can see the plates on the table of the couple that just left and thinking, "those fries still look pretty good." Good places to dumpster-dive are at grocery stores, restaurants and fast-food chains, bakeries, and convenient stores. After they close, a lot of these places will toss out still-wrapped sandwiches and food just a day after its expiration date. Do a little reconnaissance, noting which places dump their garbage when, and you can have a steady source.

Since dumpsters are usually located on private property, there is the distinct possibility that local laws in your area prohibit your visit to the D-Mart. If you don't care and are willing to take the risk, do it carefully and don't make a mess. Note: *Never* go through hospital waste. The last thing you need is to get jabbed by somebody's used needle. And beware of broken glass. Also, when you dive, be aware of the local critters you might encounter. Raccoons love dumpsters. So do rats, spiders, and snakes. It wouldn't hurt to wear long sleeves, pants, and heavy gloves while rummaging. A headlamp comes in very handy here.

HUNTING

Old-time hobos would sometimes eat just about anything they could get their hands on, and hobos stumbling into a jungle late at night wouldn't be too surprised to hear "possum" when they asked what that was strung up on a stick over the fire. And "squirrel" wouldn't have thrown anyone for a loop, either.

Because the basic idea is that you're not traversing the Alaskan interior in fur boots with a rifle hell bent on seceding from the Union. If you are having fantasies of going all Middle Ages–style and sitting around a fire eating roast meat off the bone and making a mess, it's probably going to stay a fantasy. However, if, under some strange circumstance you do manage to catch yourself a squirrel or a possum, or in a wild, uninhibited, return-to-nature moment you lie in wait and at just the right time leap on the back of a deer and plunge your knife into its neck, or you get jumped by a bear and serendipitously fall on your back and discover your Swiss Army knife was open and ended up in the beast's heart, by all means try your hand at turning the situation into dinner.

And Then There's Roadkill

There are those who, perhaps for bragging rights or just for shock value, claim to eat roadkill. If you have been lost in the Sierras for three weeks and are on the verge of true starvation and for some reason you're able to discover roadkill that was clearly hit by a vehicle but for whatever reason haven't had the same luck yourself in encountering a vehicle, perhaps then you might consider scraping this bit off the pavement and throwing it over your fire. Other than that, it's just not a smart idea. Unless you've got a feel for it, it's not so easy to determine time of death. And since you didn't see it before impact, you'll have no idea whether it was moving like an animal that was already sick. Also, it doesn't take long for flies or bacteria to start in on it before you've come across it, and the list can just go on and on.

Still, one could make the argument that if you are already prepared for dumpster diving, why draw the line at fresh roadkill? If this is your philosophy, be sure to at least adhere to the following.

TESTING YOUR ROADKILL'S FRESHNESS FACTOR

* Can you move its limbs easily as if the animal is just asleep? If not, rigor mortis has set in, and you can be pretty sure that the animal is at least a few hours dead. This is one dinner better left untouched.
* Don't take seconds. If there are signs that insects and flies have already had the first helping, skip it.

It might not be the first thing that comes to mind when thinking about cooking up roadkill, but different states actually have laws regarding what you can and can't do with it. In Wisconsin, for example, if you hit a deer (unlikely as a hobo), you can take it with you if you get permission, but if you hit a turkey or a bear, the state has to make a decision whether it wants to keep it or sell it. Illinois has a law that if you hit a deer with your car and kill it, and leave the scene of the accident without taking the deer, any Illinois citizen can take it provided he documents and keeps a personal record of where the animal parts are kept until it's eaten. There you go.

If you do try this, and are blown away by the results and think you just pulled off something too incredible for the rest of the world not to know about, you might want to make Marlinton, West Virginia, one of your next destinations for the Pocahontas County Roadkill Cook-Off. Here you can put your concoction up against others such as squirrel gravy over biscuits. The 2009 winning recipe was entitled "South-of-the-border Mishap," and used armadillo.

WASHING YOUR POTS AND PANS AND DISHES AND WHATEVER ELSE

Most people would probably agree that washing dishes without a dishwasher is a pain in the ass, and trying to wash them without unlimited water and instant hot water is even more of one. The conventional washing-the-dishes-while-camping method is to use three bins, where you fill one with boiled water and a touch or two of dish soap, another with hot water but no soap, and a third with just cold water.

1. Scrape off any leftover food and place the dirty cookware/plates/utensils into the first bin and scrub, scrub, scrub.
2. Transfer them into the second tub where you give a rinsing and work off most of the soap. Finally, put them in the third bin where you give them a final rinse.

This works awesome if your car is within a few hundred feet, the river (or spigot) is just to your left, and you don't plan to hoof all of these bins on your back for six months. So you'll need to adjust to your surroundings a bit.

One thing that makes washing dishes and pans unnecessary is not to use them. If you've had enough of granola out of the bag and are ready for some hot coffee in lieu of cold water, think strategically and use as few dishes as possible (which may not be too tricky given that you probably only have one or two to begin with). If you use dishes, that whole idea of getting stuck in a food coma and waiting until the next day to wash them won't fly here unless you want to make the chore way more difficult. Best to clean up immediately after dinner, which doesn't give the food time to harden on your cookware. When you're ready to start, here's what's up.

If you're nearby a water source, take your pot there, fill it with some water, take it back with you, put your utensils in it, then take a dash of your liquid soap and swish it all around a bunch, give it a quick rinse with some fresh water, and you're done.

If you're not near water, you want to use as little of the water you have as you can. If you're using one pot/mug to both cook and eat out of, water-based foods are the easiest to clean. Add a splash of hot water, swish around, if you need to add another splash, swish, then lay it aside to dry.

If you've run out of soap or are just about down to the dregs and are hoping for a bath the following day, you can clean your pots with a little water and some sand, mud, or ash from the fire. To use the ash, take whatever's handy and scoop some of the hot coals and ash into the dirty pot. Add just enough water to make a good goop, and then drop your dirty utensils into the pot. Let it sit for a few minutes, and then using the coals as a scrubber, proceed to scrub. Then rinse with water.

"Aha!" you say, "but it's winter and totally snowing and freezing and there's no way in hell I'm going to be sticking my hands in any water." As before, first line of defense is not to even use any dishes, but if you do have a dirty pot or two, as soon as you've finished with the meal, toss some snow in, scrub it around, then splash a little boiling water in, swirl, and dump. Good to go.

With your hobo digs in fine form, your belly full, and your dishes clean, it's time to start thinking about making some money here and there so you can maintain your new lifestyle.

⚠ REMEMBER: When you're out there on your own and without a home, two things you've up until now probably taken for granted—finding things to eat and a place to sleep for the night—are gonna be right up there on your to-do list. But with some skills, an open mind, perseverance, and maybe a visit or two to the D-Mart, you'll quickly learn to make your home wherever you are.

Did You Know Jack London Hoboed?

Best known for writing *Call of the Wild* and *White Fang*, Jack London also served his time traveling as a hobo, and later immersed himself in London's East End living among the poor to better understand the conditions under which they lived, writing about it in *The People of the Abyss*. He was born John Griffith Chaney in 1876 in San Francisco. When his father learned John's mother was pregnant, he demanded she end the pregnancy, and when she wouldn't, he refused any and all responsibility for the baby that would come. Devastated, while still pregnant John's mother shot herself—but survived. After he was born she gave him up and he was raised by a foster mother, an ex-slave. A year later, when his mother married a Civil War veteran, John London, she took her baby back.

He was working in a cannery by the age of thirteen, and by sixteen borrowed some money from his foster mother, purchased a boat, and became an oyster pirate. East coast oysters were in high demand at the time and were brought to California over the transcontinental railroad and transplanted and grown in artificial beds on land owned by the Southern Pacific Railroad. The growers' monopoly on the oysters led to excessive prices, and under the cover of night, the "pirates" would raid the beds and sell the oysters at the Oakland markets the following morning. There was a lot of resentment toward the railroads, and the pirates were seen as American Robin Hoods. In his teens he changed his name to Jack.

At the start of his hobo days and in the opening to *The Road*, London describes the scene in Reno, Nevada, in 1902, where a "horde" of hungry hobos went around banging on people's back doors until the people stopped answering them. In his own attempt to get some food, he went to one house and when he noticed the wife standing behind her husband, he figured he might get some sympathy. He asked the husband for something to eat and was challenged to work for it by moving bricks. They ended up getting into a philosophical debate centering on what kind of person Jack was and how he was unlike the homeowner. Jack asked if he should try to be more like the husband, who said yes, he should. To which London replied that if everyone were just like him, there wouldn't be anyone to move his bricks.

London rode freight trains east, finally arriving in Niagara Falls. He slept in a field that night, and in the morning, while walking into town, he was accosted by a police officer who quickly identified him as a "tramp" and marched him straight to jail. Along with a slew of other hobos, London was hauled into court, where the judge went right down the line, asking what the charge was. Each time the charge was vagrancy, and each time he sentenced the hobo to thirty days in the penitentiary, which is what London received. Adding insult to injury, London tells that one of the men, when questioned by the judge as to the reason for his vagrancy, answered that he had lost his job. The judge then gave him another thirty days for losing it.

CHAPTER 5

Getting By

"REAL"-WORLD CONSIDERATIONS

"A man who leaves home to mend himself and others is a philosopher; but he who goes from country to country, guided by the blind impulse of curiosity, is a vagabond."

OLIVER GOLDSMITH,
IN *THE CITIZEN OF THE WORLD*

Unless you have something set up before you hop that first freight car or have an uncle that knows a guy who knows a guy that knows a guy who has some work for you, you're going to have to find it. Although you've probably only thought about how you'll be logging a few thousand miles cruising the countryside or winding through the mountains on a freight train taking pictures of yourself looking every bit the desperado . . . at some point you're going to have to get down to business and earn a few bucks.

Looking through a deli storefront window with an empty belly and without a nickel to chew on while people inside casually take monstrous bites out of a sub can just about split your brain in half. Look at this as one of the sacrifices you've made to have your freedom, and remind yourself that subs always look better than they taste anyway. Maybe in the past you thought that "the man" was the one keeping you down and making your life miserable. But now you can't help but see that he was also providing a paycheck, health insurance, a place to go every day, gas for the car, and some sort of structure for your life. Yes, life without "the man" can be great. You can stand outside an office building at 9:15 in the morning in whatever T-shirt you like making faces at the people inside. On the other hand, when it drops to twenty degrees and you're still in that T-shirt because anything warmer costs money you don't have, you have to admit "the man" makes life easier.

So now you need some work. It may seem like tedium and exactly the kind of thing you'd hoped to escape by tossing yourself in a boxcar in the first place, and it can be—stacking boxes in someone's dusty attic when it's a hundred degrees and all you have to look forward to is a thin mattress on the floor and oatmeal in the morning probably wasn't one of your objectives—but it can also be a critical part of your adventure (and not of too little importance if you hope to be eating something more exciting than beans and rice—or even just beans and rice, for that matter).

WHERE TO FIND WORK

Before you can even begin to complain about how hot and dusty it is and that all you're getting in return is a nasty place to sleep, you've got to find that job. When it comes to this part of hoboing, you may have thought all you needed to do was hang out at the local bar long enough and some stranger would walk in, size up the place, spot you, march over, and offer you a job because you look like the kind of person who could do it. And this could happen, depending on the state of the other people at the bar at that particular moment and if his needs require him to walk out the door with an employee, but it's a long shot. And unless you feel like walking barefoot or can find someone crazy enough to buy your liquid soap, you don't have anything to sell. Therefore, most likely, you'll have to put your mind to the test and sleuth out the work.

Without rent, a mortgage, utility bills, car payments, and whatever else necessitates a steady stream of income, you're at a distinct advantage. All you need is to every so often hear someone say something to the effect of, "Yeah, I might just have something, why don't you swing by," and you've got a few bucks in your pocket to carry you through to another day.

Online

Craigslist cannot be beat for this type of thing. Nothing even comes close to it. Looking under the "gigs" section, in cities and towns across the United States, you will find a plethora of work options to keep your pockets full enough to put food in the belly, get you a book to read, and set you on your way to your next destination. You'll find everything from people needing help with their move for a few hours to people who need a door or window replaced.

Temp Agencies

This can be tricky because you won't have a home address (if you're staying put for an extended period of time, you could rent a PO box from the post office), but if you know someone who lives where you currently are, you can ask him if you can use his. If you leave town before a payday, your friend can then mail the check to you when you're set up in your next destination. If you have an account at a nationwide bank, you can deposit the check into your account. If you don't, you can suck it up and take it to one of those rip-off check-cashing places that specialize in getting you your money quick under the condition that they get to keep a chunk of it, too.

Local Bulletin Boards

Lots of great temporary gigs are posted here. Look in the Laundromat, hardware store, grocery store, public library, and town hall to find people looking for everything from someone to paint a shed to someone to haul firewood for a few days.

Newspapers

Looking for jobs through the local paper might seem like an outdated idea—and it is—but in smaller towns this is still often the main way people advertise. True, people probably aren't going to post an ad in the paper that they need someone to mow their lawn tomorrow, but you don't know what you might be missing unless you look.

Hit the Streets

Find a business or shop, walk in, and see if they need help with anything, making it clear that you're not looking for anything permanent. They could have a large shipment out back, for example, that they need unloaded and are more than happy to give someone ten bucks to do it, or a couple hundred flyers they need folded and stuffed into envelopes.

Talk to People

Go places where people congregate and just mingle. Think parks, coffee houses, etc. You can try this at bars too, where after a few drinks people can start feeling a little more generous, but just be careful you don't get suckered in and end up drinking away all the money you do have only to ask the question toward the end of the drinking session and hear them say, "Oh, I don't have any work right now."

Day Labor

Lots of town and cities have day labor sites where you can go, hang for the day, and hope to be picked up for a day's work, and you get paid the same day. If things go well you might get another day or two out of it, potentially even more, but the main point is even if you go five days in a week and only get one job out of it, you'll have made enough to feed yourself for a few weeks.

HOW TO SECURE WORK

Just because you've given up possession of an address doesn't mean all the rules for everyone else have changed. For the most part, the aspects of finding a job back in the "real world" apply here as well. You still need to know how to approach and talk to people, how to present yourself in a positive light, and how—even when the job is temporary—to project the impression you'll see the job through. Anyone who has come before you and taken a job only to split town with half the job done because he "just felt like it" has stacked the deck against you. When you are given the benefit of the doubt and someone agrees to give you some cash—or a place to stay—in exchange for some commitment on your part, follow through. You'll like yourself better for it in the end, and when the next optimistic "Angelina" saunters in fresh from the rails looking for some work, he may benefit from your good conduct.

Angelina: A young kid without any experience. "Had to point out to this Angelina the reason his train wasn't leaving the yard was because it wasn't even on a track."

You need to talk to people, and a lot of people. And you need to be unabashedly clear that you're looking for a little work, a day's worth or even just a few hours, and someone, eventually, will hook you up. You need to keep at it even after you've been shot down ten, twenty, thirty times. There are some things working in your favor. One is that you don't need to make a lot of money, just enough to get by and make it to your next point of interest, so unless they're asking you to do something for free, you have the flexibility to make a deal and don't have to waste a lot of time trying to squeeze them for every last penny.

You're also not looking for a career, you're either looking to do something you have skills for that the person hiring you doesn't, or you're going to do something for that person that they don't want to do themselves. And everyone with a house has more than a few things they need done that they don't want to do themselves and would be happy to give someone a couple bucks to do. That's the great thing about what you're looking to do.

Regardless of the type of job you're looking for, it's best not to show up at any of these places looking for work with your bindle in full bloom and your face looking like you just took a dust bath. Bust out your glad rags, leave the bag at "home," and go in looking tight. Your odds will be a lot better. It's also best not to lie, or to lie as little as possible.

glad rags: The best set of clothes a hobo has and keeps clean for those occasions when presentation is key, like when trying to get a job. "Damn, I'm lookin' tight with these glad rags."

SEASONAL JOBS—VACATION, RECREATION, AND THE HOLIDAY SPIRIT

The days of working and living like you just walked out of the *Grapes of Wrath* have been forever changed, but there are still seasonal jobs available, and once you open your mind to it, you'll see that there are actually many more seasonal jobs than there were in the past. Who got paid to make fake snow in a Laredo, Texas, parking lot so little kids could snowboard for a few feet in back in 1896?

Cold Months

If you ski, and ski well (or can at least make it look good), dig up any connections you may have and see if you can land a ski instructor position for the winter. You could also just show up with a pair of skis and act like you know what you're doing—but that usually only works in movies. Forget major resorts, as they tend to hire people who are a bit more "professional," but smaller operations need help too (*someone* needs to teach kids how to snow plow). Just because they don't have 5,000 vertical feet like they do in Colorado and Tahoe doesn't mean you can't go skiing in Wisconsin. Even if you can't ski, resorts also have any number of jobs to fill, ranging from working in the food service to the rental shops to snow making. Dig deep.

Particularly during the winter, places like UPS and FedEx hire temporary help to keep up with holiday volume, and department stores also often need wrappers around the same time.

> Be a hobo entrepreneur. Find a buddy, rent a U-haul, go to a tree farm in the country and buy a bunch. Bring them back to an urban area and sell them out of the back of your truck. As with any entrepreneurial endeavor, this involves risk. You need some upfront capital to buy the trees to begin with, and you need to do a little assessment of demand before you purchase twenty trees and get stuck with fifteen Douglas firs and an additional sixty gallons of diesel you don't need.

When some cities get a huge snowfalls that really clogs things up, they will sometimes put out a call looking for a temporary labor force to help shovel. Weird, but true. Take advantage of it.

Warm Months

The summer provides opportunities along the same lines. Ever been a camp counselor? Think you could be? Like kids? Try and plan ahead and see if you rustle up a position. Surf? Get yourself to a beach and offer lessons. Doesn't need to consist of anything more formal than offering. During the summer season, as well, parks will often need people to man the parking kiosks, maintain trails, and keep the bathrooms clean. As an added boon, you can often find a good place to camp not too far from "work."

Another option where you can really live it up is on cruise ships. They often need help as well in food service and hospitality.

beachcomber: When a hobo spends most of his time on the waterfront, he's a beachcomber.

The Final Frontier

If hopping freight cars and hitching rides with strangers and a few nights sleeping on cardboard in an old caboose have proven to you that you can keep company with anyone and you're in no need of glamour, go to Alaska and land a seasonal job in the fishing industry. You probably won't want to look at another fish for the rest of your life, but the pay can be decent, you'll get in shape, you'll have a place to stay, and the memories and the smell in your nostrils will last you the rest of your life. Previous experience not needed, as anyone who already had some probably wouldn't be looking to gain any more.

But Alaska, for whatever reason—perhaps their lack of a large population—can be an amazing source of employment. They're constantly advertising for people to help with the parks, tours, lodges, and cruise lines.

Agriculture

Industrial farming has put many a hobo out of work. Machines have reduced the amount of labor in some cases down to the few people who operate the machinery. But even though machines have eliminated the need for armies of temporary workers, they haven't completely obliterated seasonal jobs working in agriculture. Additionally there are a few groups, some international, such as WWOOF, that arrange relationships between organic farms and volunteers who, in return for a set number of hours of work, receive free food and lodging. A little bit like the old days. But remember, going up to a farmer in the Midwest and asking if he needs help harvesting the wheat is a bit like bringing a club to a gunfight. Useless. Finally, if you plan on looking for agricultural work, make sure you show up in the right place at the right time; hoping to make some money in Minnesota during the apple season but arriving in St. Paul during May will leave you picking more pocket lint than anything else.

Faced with a labor shortage in the 1950s, the California tomato harvest was threatened. While mechanized harvesting had been tried, it usually resulted in spaghetti sauce, as the tomatoes were consequently crushed in the process. In response, researchers at UC Davis developed the "square tomato," which solved the problem. Though not really square, machines could pick them, and because they weren't completely round, they didn't fall off conveyor belts, and survived transportation. The "parents" of these tough tomatoes were chosen through the following test: A farmer went through the fields, picked up random tomatoes, and threw them into the road. If the tomato survived, they were bred further, if they didn't, no babies for them.

ROUGH PICKING SEASON GUIDELINES

* Tomato picking happens in central California, a bit near the Great Lakes, and some in the Northeast.
* Peppers, being in love with the heat, spring up in the South.
* People still pick pears and apples; think late summer. Apples are mostly grown in Washington state and New York.
* Oranges are mainly grown in the South, and the same with peaches.
* Most table grapes, those you eat in bunches and find in the grocery store, are grown east of the Mississippi and from Canada south to Florida. Wine grapes, on the other hand, are in northern and central California, and in Oregon, mostly in late fall. And in addition to picking the grapes, wineries often need help with the processing. They don't turn into wine by themselves.

road stake: The amount of money a hobo makes while working out on the road. Traditionally a hobo might work the summer months to get up a large enough stake that he could then live on for the winter in hobohemia.

The animal farming industry such as dairy farms, ranching, chickens, and so on are not seasonal, run throughout the year, and often need labor help. If you're lucky, you can even get to ride a horse and do your best *Lonesome Dove* interpretation. Again, your best bet for finding farm work doesn't involve showing up at the largest commercial farm outside of Des Moines. Look for smaller, mom-and-pop-style farms. While walking down the road, if you see someone riding a tractor, walk right up and ask if he needs any help. He might give you some work and let you sleep in the barn or at least throw your tent up somewhere on his 165 acres. And you never know, he may even put you up in your own room and give you a fresh pair of boots when he sees the condition of yours.

Good Work If You Can Get It

It boils down to this: Ask yourself what skills you have, and then try to capitalize on them. Can you craft, sew, type, repair stuff, haul stuff, cook? You would be surprised at what can happen, because just like in the heyday of the hobo, there are plenty of people and businesses who only need a day or two of help, and while that does nothing for a "regular" job seeker, it's a lifeline for a temporary worker, as you probably only need a few days to restock the ol' wallet. After all, you're not trying to fill a bank account (though should the opportunity present itself . . .), and you probably don't really want to stick around much longer than that anyway. It's good for both of you.

barnacle: In the eyes of a hobo, anyone who has stayed with the same job for more than a year or has been in the same place for a long time. Long enough to be compared to a barnacle.

Which is what you've got going for you. You've don't need much. Look at the cost of things. You're living essentially for free, you don't have any utilities to pay for; all you need is enough cash to purchase some critical supplies.

BANKS

Realistically speaking, it's hard to get by without a bank account, a place to put your money other than just in your wallet or a Ziploc bag. You probably already have one and should consider keeping it as you hit the road. ATMs can be super convenient, provided you're using one that belongs to your bank. Otherwise you end up paying anywhere from five to ten dollars for taking out twenty. To avoid this, get an account with a large national bank that has ATMs all over the place. Makes it easier to do everything—make deposits and get money, even buy supplies when you don't have any cash.

STRETCHING THE DOLLAR

You might wonder, given the knowledge that you could blow $50 on dinner for two in an instant, how long you could live off it when you're not buying lattes. There are a variety of ways to tighten your money belt.

stamp collectors: People collecting food stamps in several cities along a rail line.

HOARDING PENNIES

* When you shop for supplies, check out the circulars most places keep near their entrances. You'll often find some pretty amazing deals, particularly when they end up with an overstock of some item. How much tuna can you eat? Maybe a lot when it's twenty-five cents a can.
* If you have an expensive coffee habit, kill it. Starbucks can turn an already thin wallet into an emaciated one.
* A smoker? There has never been a better time to quit. You can keep one on you to smoke in that dramatic moment when you get pinned between two train cars and feel your life slowly

waning, but otherwise, you'll be beating yourself over the head the next time you run out of money and realize you've spent $75 on smokes since you left home.

* Bars will also kill your wallet. A better method is to buy your beer at the grocery store or convenience store and bring it back to camp with you or wherever it is you're staying. If you're more into the social scene than the drinking scene, hang at the bar but limit the drinking.
* Buy generic whenever possible.

Stretch your money to the breaking point, where you've gotten so much out of that dollar and squeezed it so dry it's no longer worth anything, then—and only then—should you think about starting in on another one. We live in the most consumer-driven society in the world, and trying to reprogram yourself is no simple task. You're like a guy finding his sea legs, except that you're on land and you're trying to learn how to walk around without spending any money. You need to save everything you can for what's coming up ahead. There's nothing like spending a couple dollars on an unnecessary impulse buy only to later come across something you really need, like bus fare, but you're thirty cents shy. That just sucks.

Everybody always wants more; it's the way we're conditioned. You are now conditioning yourself to survive on less and be happy with what you've got. This will take some discipline.

Since every possible thing you come across has been monetized, this is actually a fairly simple endeavor. Look for what you want, then buy the one that's the cheapest. If you're thirsty, go for the drink that doesn't have anything special going on, as "special" always costs something. For example if you're going to buy soda, consider seltzer, and the generic brand at that. At which point ask yourself, why don't I just drink some water? You just saved yourself some money.

And when you think to yourself, as you undoubtedly will as you try to rationalize the purchase of something, "Whatever, it's like, $1.39," add that up a few times. Then in a week, after you've saved yourself from nine or ten soda purchases, you'll look down, discover your socks are toast, and realize you can buy a fresh three-pack of socks with the soda money you would have spent to keep those fancy Super Bowl ads on the air.

> ▲ **REMEMBER:** Sooner or later your new freewheeling countryside roaming way o' life will scream out for some financing. You can achieve this pretty much any way you can except for sitting in the middle of the woods just thinking about it. Get out there and do it.

Did You Know George Orwell Hoboed?

Eric Allan Blair, who is known more by his pen name, George Orwell, and for his books *Animal Farm* and *1984*, was born in 1903. As a teenager he read Jack London's *The People of the Abyss*, was inspired, and later followed suit: He decided to live as a tramp, dressed the part, adopted the lifestyle, and traveled through society's underbelly, working odd jobs, and later wrote *Down and Out in London and Paris* about his experiences. He spent time in England's workhouses, picked hops, washed dishes, and worked in a bookstore where he became so disgusted with customers that he started to hate the books as well.

After hearing hop picking romanticized by other writers (most likely not any who had done it themselves), in 1931 Orwell thought to give it a shot. He set out with four others, traveling from farm to farm looking for jobs, camping out in the fields, and when the weather was bad spending the night in a "spike," a building where the tramps were kept separate from the main building of the workhouse. When they finally did arrive at the hop farm, Orwell found nothing romantic about it. He wrote to a friend that he and three other workers were given accommodations in a tin hopper hut, with open windows that let in the weather, and no furniture other than hay.

In the same letter, Orwell shared some things that he had learned while tramping: That to get rid of the smoky taste water could get from being boiled over a fire, you could put a wood chip into the water, that when sleeping outside it was warmer to lay your coat over yourself as a blanket than wear it, and that the best time to beg meat from a butcher was on Saturday nights.

And in an interesting parallel to what was going on at the same time with the American hobo, he added as a postscript that he had yet to come across any of the markings he had heard tramps would leave to communicate what you could expect at any given house, and thought that the practice must have been discontinued because none of the tramps he had spoken to were aware of such a system. But perhaps some of the best advice given to Orwell during his travels came from Boris, a traveling companion. Both looking for work, Orwell noted to Boris that he looked pale, to which Boris replied, "Curse it, what can one do on bread and potatoes? It is fatal to look hungry. It makes people want to kick you."

CHAPTER 6

Getting Going (Again)

A WISE HOBO IS A HAPPY HOBO

"When you get to a fork in the road, take it."

—YOGI BERRA

As you make your way, on top of many of the other challenges you're facing, a fairly large one can be staying clean, from getting the dirt off your face to getting the grass stains out of your pants, things that were once fairly simple can now seem epic. Little obstacles can eventually add up to some serious need to kvetch, and kvetching to yourself can be pretty unrewarding. It can be really nice to, at some point, break up your solitude by finding like-minded people to share your trials and tribulations with, and hear theirs in return. They're out there, and they can be your new community.

KEEPING CLEAN SHOWERING—OR SOMETHING CLOSE TO IT

Chances are a hot shower each day followed by a thick cotton towel is a routine you left behind. But there are still options. The most basic, which takes almost zero time, is to use wet wipes and rubbing alcohol. With this method you can pretty much clean yourself off without having to remove your clothes (perfect for really cold days and times when privacy is nonexistent), and your smell and appearance are immediately improved.

In the Wild

If water is available and the temperature isn't too cold, go for a swim. Take your soap in with you (use a biodegradable brand to avoid polluting the water) and go at it. You could start the swim with your clothes on and wash them, too, provided you have time and ample warmth for them to dry. If it's a shallow stream you can't get into, use your cup (or pot if you're traveling with cookware) as a scoop, then pour and scrub. It can be a pretty chilly experience, but it can wake you up better than coffee—and doesn't require a fire.

Public Restrooms

Moving up the scale, seek out a public restroom, where you'll have a sink, paper towels, and liquid soap at your disposal. Standing straight nude in front of the sink as people come in and out is not the idea, unless you can handle some hard glares and staring five-year-olds and a ticket for indecency. Wash your hands well with your clothes on, and then go for the face. Rejoice now if you have short hair, as all you need is a quick splash and wipe with a paper towel. Done. No one will be the wiser, and you can always pass it off as if you just needed a little wake-up water because you've been driving all night and have a long drive ahead. Take your shirt off and go for a quick underarm and chest scrub, then put your shirt back on. Lastly, if you have a washcloth you can wet it and take it into a stall where you can attack your lower sections. If not, just loosen your pants and with a minimum of water go for the groin and upper thighs. When you've finished, pull your pant leg up and do one leg a time. Same with the feet. The whole process becomes a lot simpler if you're at a restroom at odd hours when there's less traffic, or if you just take the attitude, "Whatever, I've transcended this normal stuff."

> If you happen to be traveling the highways, many truck stops have showers you can use. At $9 to $15 it's not the cheapest option, but for those times when you're really beat and feel like splurging without getting a hotel room, the service can't be beat. And this is not like a huge room with twenty showerheads where you have to avert your eyes from nineteen other people. You'll often get a private room with clean towels, soap, and shampoo.

SELF-MAINTENANCE TIPS

* Wash your hands regularly and use hand sanitizer.
* Avoid touching your face. People do this all the time without even being aware of it, and despite conventional wisdom that you get sick from getting things in your mouth, your most vulnerable parts to germs and bacteria are your eyes and nose. Try not to touch or rub them unless your hands are clean.
* Try to get a good soap bath at least every other day. This may seem impossible, but make do with what you can and push the extra bit to make it happen.
* Brush your teeth every day. Not just something your parents and dentist always bugged you about, keeping a healthy set of teeth and gums is ridiculously important to overall body health and well-being.
* Change your socks and underwear every day. Really.
* Drink only boiled, purified, or iodized water unless you don't mind a mean case of the runs or something worse, like giardia. Don't just drink from a stream, lake, or pond thinking that just because it's out in "nature" means that it's untainted. Most of it is. You can be drinking downstream from everything from an outhouse to a factory to a leaky septic system. Purify it.
* Wash foraged foods (with purified water) before eating them.
* Make sure your eating utensils are clean.
* Avoid sunburn by gradually developing a tan. If you will be in the sun long, wear a hat with a brim and a panel in the back to protect your neck.
* Avoid heat stroke by resting during the hottest part of the day (midday).

Your Clothes

Prepare for a change if you're used to going a week or two without doing laundry: Funk is your new enemy. You're only going to have a few pairs of socks, shirts, and underwear, and traveling as you are, they're going to get dirty. Really dirty. If you have any hopes of visiting a coffee shop in town or picking up some work, you'll need to keep a clean set of clothes around, your "glad rags." For a quick wash you need only a decent-sized plastic bag without holes, some water, and your Dr. Bronner's. Here's how to wash your clothes on the run:

1. Fill your plastic bag with some water and squeeze a bit of Dr. Bronner's into it.
2. Drop in your dirty clothes, rub them together, and swish them all around.
3. Let them sit for ten minutes.
4. Pull them out, pour out the dirty water, and refill the bag with clean water.
5. Put your clothes back in, rinse them well, and then wring them well.

Now you can make your own jungle, build a fire, wash your clothes, and feed yourself. If you haven't already, it's high time you went out and tried to find your tribe.

HOBO SYMBOLS

Vagrancy laws being what they were, early hobos arriving in a new place without much information as to where to go were pretty vulnerable. Unknowingly knocking on the door of a judge's house, for example, while looking for work, could be a setback. When other hobos, unaware of the first hobo's experience, proceeded to make the same mistake, the problem became clear. They needed a way to spread information. Therefore, they developed a code of symbols so they could communicate with one other. That they were symbols as opposed to words took care of another problem: Many hobos were illiterate. Today, while you may still come across meaningful hobo symbols here and there, most of the writing you'll find consists of basic "I was here" declarations, as opposed to "Tell this woman a sob story and she'll give you food."

Still, nothing says "seasoned" so well as being able to talk about the way it was, and you may still find occasion where the knowledge can be useful. If you have some people meeting up with you, but they're a few days behind, leaving a quick drawing that will eventually wash off with the rain so as not to cause any vandalism may be more effective than trying to describe, "and then you'll see, like a bush, with little tiny berries, turn there . . ."

Likewise, if you've met another hobo on his way to a town you'll be heading to after the job you're on now ends, he can theoretically lead you through a place you've never been simply by strategically placing symbols. The whole idea is to be inconspicuous and temporary; you're not advertising a Father's Day chicken barbecue, and you should only really draw the attention of those who know what they're looking for.

Hobo codes could differ by region of the country, and would change over time if it seemed citizens were beginning to catch on to them. If you want to leave a message, you can form a fairly meaningful message through different combinations, such as "Don't go that way, a guy with a gun and a really mean dog lives there, but over this way is a nice old lady who will set you up if you give her a sad story."

Don't bother going this way

Go this way

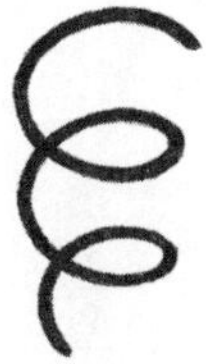

A judge lives here

This place is not safe

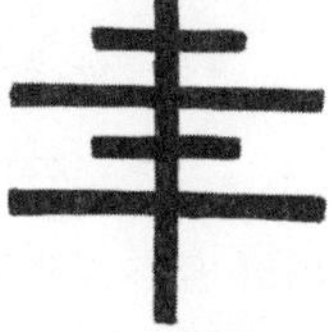

Officer of the law lives here

Not safe here; crime committed

Kind woman lives here;
tell pitiful story

Dishonest person lives here

Nothing to be gained here

Rich people live here

Good place for a handout

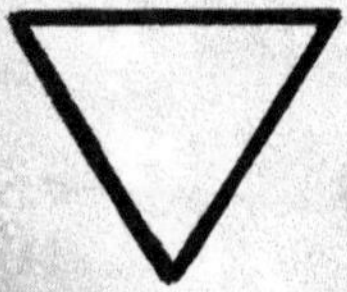

This road is spoiled; full of other hobos

This is a well guarded house

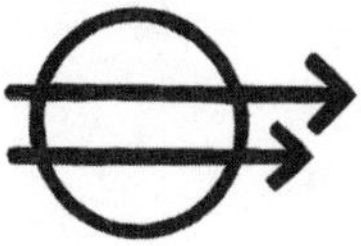
Hit the road! Quick!

The owner is out

The authorities here are alert

Fresh water; safe campsite

Jail

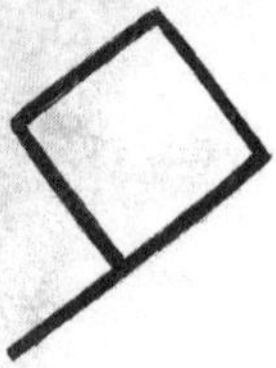

Hold your tongue

Be prepared to defend yourself

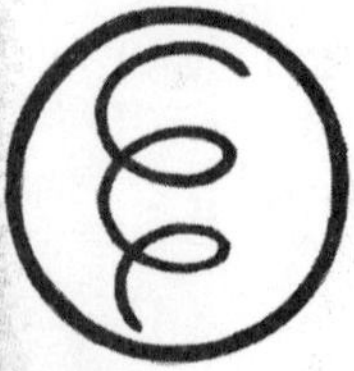

Courthouse; precinct station

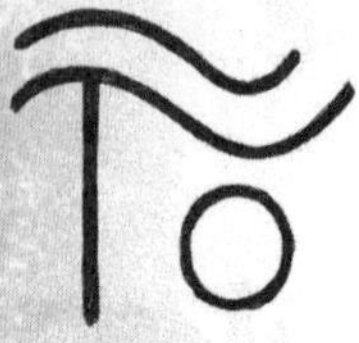

You can sleep in the hayloft

This is the place

Alcohol in this town

Gentleman lives here

People here indifferent to hobos

Vicious dog here

Religious talk gets free meal

Okay, all right

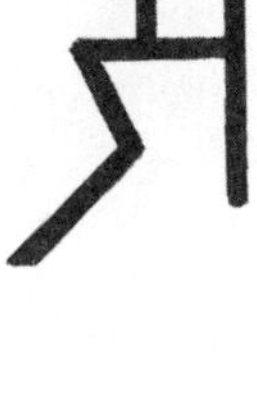

Food here if you work

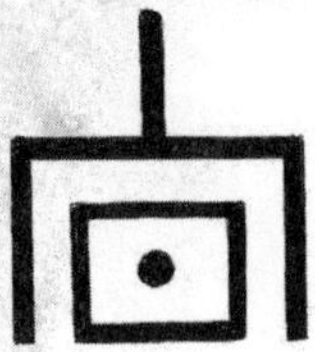

Dangerous neighborhood

Police here frown on hobos

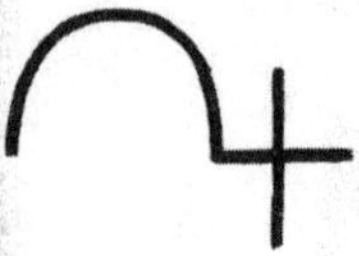

Halt

This is a good road to follow

Doubtful

You can camp here

Man with a gun lives here

There are thieves here

The sky is the limit

Dangerous drinking water

Trolley stop

Good place to catch a train

Barking dog lives here

Doctor here won't charge

A beating awaits you here

Ill-tempered man lives here

TALKING THE TALK: LANGUAGE SKILLS

Sitting around a jungle with a bunch of hobos trash talking and telling war stories, you can feel pretty out of place when you're only picking up the meaning of three out of every five words spoken. Over the past hundred years hobos have weathered a lot of circumstances unique to their lifestyle, and as a consequence developed some new words, and new meanings for old words, in order to best convey what went down. If no interpreter is available, it can be helpful to get some choice words lodged in your brain so not only will you understand what's being said, but you can prattle away in your own right. Aside from the ones you've already found throughout the book, here are a few more terms to learn:

Bindlestiff: A hobo with his bindle.

"Bo": Short for "hobo," used by a hobo to refer to another. "That 'bo best duck or he's liable to lose his head."

Bone polisher: A vicious dog.

Bone orchard: A graveyard.

Bullets: Beans that weren't cooked right and are still hard. Might not kill you, but not all that pleasant, either.

C, H, and D: What someone might say if he's cold, hungry, and thirsty. The "D" is for dry. "Yo 'bo, I'm C, H, and D."

Cover with the moon: To sleep out in the open.

Elevated: To be under the influence of drugs or booze.

Flop: A place to sleep. Hotels on skid row and just plain old cheap ones in general were known as "Flophouses." Not where anyone of means took his family while on vacation.

Frisco circle: Method used by hobos to take up a communal collection. Draw a circle on the ground, everyone who wants to partake of what's to be bought throws their change into the pot.

Gump: Refers to a meat scrap, as in, "Hey, toss that gump into the mulligan."

Hooch: Alcohol.

Jungle buzzard: (1) A hobo who steals from other hobos. (2) A hobo who hangs around the jungles while living off others but never contributing.

Moniker/Monica: The nickname given to a hobo, such as "Buffalo Slim," or "Pancake Papa." Usually chosen because it describes either the hobo, where he's from, or something he did or does. "Given your cooking ability, I'm thinking something like, 'Tennessee Bullets' oughta fit."

Mulligan: Time-honored hobo stew. Made from whatever the hobos present in the jungle at that particular time have to offer.

Padding the hoof: Traveling by foot.

Possum belly: To ride on top a passenger car. The hobo has to lie flat on his stomach, like an action hero on the roof of a car, to keep from being thrown off.

Punk: Any young kid

Reefer: A refrigerator car.

Sky pilot: A preacher or minister.

LIFE IN THE JUNGLES

Perhaps up to this point you've been camping by yourself or staying with friends, family, or even on the occasional random couch. If during your travels you come across some other hobos, which you inevitably will, they may clue you in to the locations of some active jungles. You probably will have already seen long-abandoned jungle cemeteries.

These can be your homes away from home—as well as perfect places to commiserate about life on the road with other like-minded individuals full of good information. A robust jungle filled with kind people is a welcome panacea to a hard life on the road. Generally located near enough to the railroad so as to be convenient but far enough away so as not to attract too much attention, an ideal hobo location is also close to a water source to make cooking and cleaning convenient, and hopefully has enough wood around to keep the fire going. As you approach, weary, thirsty, and hungry, you'll experience the relief of "calling in" and getting your batteries recharged. This is where you can find the true spirit of the hobo. Communal caring. This can be much needed, particularly when you've had a recent rough spell of hard traveling, no work, no money, no company, or some mixture of all of them.

calling in: When a hobo comes in and shares another hobo's campfire.

Since you'll be hanging out with other hobos, this could even be your lucky day when you acquire your moniker. After a long night of spilling your guts and spinning your yarns, out of the blue, someone—although he may have just tuned in to the last of your story—may suddenly utter the words that will come to define you for the rest of your hobo travels. Hopefully, it won't be something like, "shifty bastard," or "ass backwards." You'll probably meet a number of people whose monikers you've already come across. You'll learn of the places to go and the places to avoid, where you can catch a few nights sleep and a few days work. You can also meet up with folks more experienced on the road than you, who may take you under their wing and show you the ropes.

Since this is "home," creating and maintaining a communal environment for safe and supportive living is the main goal. Make sure you do your part to keep it operating smoothly. You'll undoubtedly come across "jungle buzzards," people taking advantage of other people's hard work and contributing nothing in return. Make sure you don't become one of them. Today we have all sorts of names for these kinds of people: moochers, freeloaders, leeches, takers, etc. None of them are too flattering.

Today, jungles often take on an unpleasant quality. They were once among the most revered places a hobo could end up, where people abided by unspoken rules that kept them relatively safe, clean, and hospitable. You didn't leave your garbage around, you didn't piss in the jungle or even right next to it—you went at least 100 feet away—everyone contributed to the mulligan, and you were free to use the cooking utensils and ware that existed as long as you cleaned them up when you were done.

Nels Anderson, an American sociologist, spent years studying hobos and the social conditions that created, sustained, and ultimately destroyed them. Intrigued by hobos and hoping to create a broader cultural understanding between them and the rest of society, in 1923 he published his research in *The Hobo: The Sociology of the Homeless Man*. He discerned several jungle rules that were never to be broken; a quick look at them and one can see they would be as apropos now as they were back then. Essentially, as he understood it, the jungle rules were as follows:

1. Don't make a fire at night that could attract attention if the authorities have been known to pay a visit in the past.
2. Don't steal from people at night while they're sleeping in the jungles. (He called this "hi-jacking.")
3. Don't allow "buzzing," or letting the jungle turn into a hospitality center for jungle buzzards who live off of other people's supplies and meal leftovers.
4. Don't waste food.
5. Do wash the cookware you use after cooking and eating.
6. Don't cook on the communal fire without doing some legwork and bringing in wood yourself.
7. Don't bust up any equipment that belongs to the jungle. In other words, if you want to leave your tools and cook stove out in the rain to get rusty, that's your business. If they belong to someone else, take care of them.

If you end up in the one of the less-than-awesome jungles, they may be filled with garbage and full of (mostly unhelpful) people who may or may not be actual "hobos" and have more interest in what's in your pack than anything else. Today, jungles are often filled with debris, whether it's old car seats with stuffing coming out or couches with the springs popping through the cushion, and the ground littered with empty cans, beer bottles, and junk food wrappers. Just because this is often the state of the modern jungle doesn't mean you should participate.

Kingsbury Run was an old riverbed running through Cleveland, Ohio. It was also the site of a large hobo jungle, and the train tracks ran through it. Just to the east was the "Roaring Third," a true depiction of hobohemia filled with flophouses, bars, brothels, and gambling dens. From 1934 to 1938, thirteen people were murdered in the area—all of them decapitated, most of them transients. As the murders went unsolved, pressure mounted on the police. At one point a hobo about to hop a train tripped over something, only to discover it was a human torso. Eliot Ness of *The Untouchables* fame was the safety director for the city. The killer soon gained the moniker, the "Mad Butcher." Frustrated, Ness went for a full-on raid of the Run at midnight in 1938. His crew started at one end and worked their way down to the other, capturing sixty-three men. When they were finished, Ness burned the jungle to the ground. Although a man was jailed for the murders (and died in jail before trial), most assume he was innocent, and the case remains unsolved.

Jungles are also nowhere near as abundant as they once were. Convenient places for jungles were near water sources and near places where trains stopped or moved slowly. In this way, jungles were kind of like hobo train depots. A prime place for jungles used to be near the water towers where steam trains had to stop in order to take on water. But as diesel locomotives took over in the thirties and trains flew by at full speed, there was no longer a reason to maintain jungles in these areas.

Around the same time, the railroads made more of a concerted effort at reducing the number of jungles, primarily the permanent ones, and have on several occasions gone through with bulldozers to further make their point.

You'll probably find yourself making your own jungles as you travel, sometimes making them with others that you meet along the way. Jungles do still exist, and your ticket in finding them will be connecting with other hobos.

THE NATIONAL HOBO CONVENTION

Since 1900, The National Hobo Convention has taken place every second weekend in August; this is kind of like the Lollapalooza for hobos—minus the massive headliners. A long weekend celebration of all things "hobo," you'll meet all manner of characters there, from old-time hobos to yuppie and recreational hobos to people who just think hobos are cool and want to hang out. It's kind of a "who's who" of hobodom, and all are welcome. Those who aren't hobos, but like the idea and enjoy exposure, are warmly referred to as "hobos at heart." But before you get too excited and become convinced you're about to enter hobo heaven, know that it might not be quite what you're expecting. Even in its first year in Britt, Iowa (previously it moved from place to place), many hobos were turned off by the "country fair" aspect of the get-together, something that has only increased over the years. Today the events include hobo 5k and 10k races, a classic car show, the hobo museum, arts and crafts, and even a boxcar on fake railroad tracks. Purists sometimes have a problem with the whole thing, finding it somewhat of a parody of what a true hobo is. While there are still some who arrive by rail, most of the attendees arrive by bus, car, and RVs. And this is not isolated to the national convention; there are hobo festivals across the country filled with hobo reenactments and re-creations of hobo jungles, with people in character fielding questions from the audience. Perhaps not your scene.

Still, you can find some old-timers in attendance as well as current hobos, and by listening and talking to people you'll add to your hobo repertoire of survival and travel knowledge—also known as "road knowledge," which on your current path can be worth more than a college education. You'll get tips on where to catch trains, what places are great for working, how to live better on the road, locations of good jungles across the country, places to watch out for, and people it might be good for you to hook up with. You'll also hear an enormous number of stories, hear hobo songs you won't hear anywhere else, and get to watch the coronation of the hobo king and queen—complete with a parade and a formal crowning ceremony. Good stuff.

There are dozens of other hobo meet-ups throughout the year, including the West Coast Hobo Gathering, the East Coast Hobo Gathering, and a lot of others that fluctuate and are planned semi-spontaneously. Best way to keep up with what's going on is by staying in contact with other hobos and by searching out Internet hobo "chatter." Find some of these and you may have the luck of hooking up with some folks more veteran than you and you'll have the benefit of receiving a great introduction to life on the road by others who have already bushwhacked the way.

DOWNTIME

Another boon to your current lifestyle is the fact that what you need pretty much matches the money you make—you don't make a lot, but you also don't need a lot. As long as you have some food, you're almost never in need of money immediately. Don't make any money for several days, or even a few weeks, and your life can still maintain an even keel, while back in the land of house and apartment dwellers, your life may start to crumble without cash. Miss a few bills and the calls and letters start coming every day. There are threats, and eventually they turn off the heat, tow your car, and when you can't afford to pick up your car, just throw more fines at you. No thanks.

As a hobo, you'll make money to live on, live on it till it runs out, and then make some more. It's still a cycle, but it's not like the rat race, where as fast as you make money it goes out and there's never any rest in between. You work, you come home, eat, go to bed, wake up, and do it all over again. Perhaps this is what you were trying to get away from. But now you live with the rise and fall of the seas.

Be prepared for a lot of downtime. Time where there's nothing to do but sit around, stare at the ground, throw some rocks around, and maybe try your hand at whittling. Most of us have become so accustomed to having to tend to the many things required to keep modern life running smoothly that we're unprepared for having nothing to do. Even when we're not doing things, we're often mentally preoccupied with things that we *should* be doing, so we end up contemplating what's supposed to happen next more than focusing on what's happening now. But now you are your own keeper. It's different from a vacation in that there is no time schedule, no departure or return date (unless you left with one). So given that you can do pretty much anything that doesn't cost a lot of money, hoboing presents a great opportunity to discover (or rediscover) what interests you.

Maybe you have books in mind that you always planned on reading, once you found the time. Well, now can be that time. Keep a journal, and keep track of the things that happen each day, and what you've been thinking about. You'll be glad you did later.

Whether you're camping or not, go out and take some long walks or hikes. Remember what you're doing, which is trying to soak up as much as possible with the time you have. Pretty much everywhere you stop will have something cool to note. Take advantage of being the sole person in charge of your time and explore your surroundings.

Write postcards and letters to family and friends. Just because you're out here on life's frontier doesn't mean you need to cut off all communication with your loved ones. Let them know what's going on. It can be a particularly good time to reconnect with people you've been out of touch with for a long time. What else do you have to do? There's always counting leaves, but why not do something for someone else?

Pick a topic and learn about it. There's probably—or not just probably, but certainly—something that you've always wanted to know more about. Teach yourself. If you don't have Internet access, next time you're near a place that does download lectures available online on topics you find interesting. Take them back into the woods with you and listen to them while you hike around, or just while you're sitting around camp.

If you're one of those people who gets all worked up when reading the paper and by the end of an article are thinking, "Man, someone needs to write a letter," do it. Write letters to the editor. It's great. You can vent—although long rants have about zero chance of getting printed—and you'll feel like you've made your point. And who knows, you could have letters of yours winding up in a paper or two.

Get involved with others living a similar lifestyle to your own. Champion the hobo cause. Find the newsgroups online, introduce yourself, and start making connections. Share your travel stories and thoughts, the places you've been and where you're going. Before long you may find you've become a real part of the community. Make the community stronger.

Besides working to make money for yourself, find places looking for temporary volunteers and help out for a day or two, and maybe longer. You may discover a cause you really care about and become part of that community. You might even find your calling and a community of people you never expected to find, through which you might suddenly feel grounded and connected. And who knows, you may even stay and start putting down roots. Being a hobo doesn't mean you've taken some oath that treats starting a life in one place as cause for excommunication. Other considerations:

* Many big cities, and some small, have a day each week where the museums are free.
* If it's summertime, look for events being held in the area where you're staying. There are almost always free festivals, music, plays, and other arty or sporty events held in parks.
* Find a café not too far from where you are with couches, Internet, and people. Hang out and meet some.

▲ **REMEMBER:** Life on the road brings with it some challenges, and finding and socializing with others treading the same path can ease the transition. Figure out some of the ground rules and you'll be well on your way. One of those challenges is to stay clean and healthy. Good hygiene will carry the day—as well as the ones that follow.

Did You Know Robert Mitchum Hoboed?

Actor Robert Mitchum was born in 1917. His father worked for the railroad and was killed in a rail yard accident in 1919. He himself took to the rails at an early age, touring the country and working a number of jobs including as a ditch digger, and at fourteen was arrested for vagrancy in Savannah, Georgia, and sentenced to work on a chain gang. According to him, he was able to escape through the swamps, and made it back home.

Mitchum and his brother, Jack (what is it with hobos and the name "Jack"?), made a trip west that is described in a biography on Mitchum by Lee Server; it could have been a movie in and of itself. In 1933, the family was facing hard times and Mitchum's mother heard that in California one could find salvation. Robert and his brother decided to head out first, and their mom packed them each a bindle. They left, telling her they would be back for her.

While one would expect hitchhiking to generally be safer than hopping a freight train, one of the rides they received involved a lot of moonshine, and when they eventually stopped for the night they were awoken by a gunfight between their "hosts" and another group of men. Afterward, they figured the trains might not be too bad after all, and they hopped one to New Orleans, and spent the night in a jungle. Here, they learned of a train heading west in the morning, and so there they went.

Robert hopped on first, but before Jack could follow he found himself held at gunpoint by a railroad bull. With the train moving, Mitchum started yelling for Jack to jump on the train, that the bull wasn't going to shoot. As Server puts it, Jack "balked, looked at the .38 staring at him, and decided that the railroad cop knew a little more about whether he would or wouldn't shoot than did brother Bob." As the train carried Mitchum west, his brother was led off by the bull. Mitchum arrived in Los Angeles riding on a boxcar, with no possessions other than what he carried in his bindle.

CHAPTER 7

Getting Out of a Jam

WAIT, WHAT? I'M ARRESTED? AND OTHER STICKY SITUATIONS

"In America camping is considered a healthy sport for Boy Scouts but a crime for mature men who have made it their vocation."

—JACK KEROUAC,
"THE VANISHING AMERICAN HOBO"

Living your life according to your own deal and not feeling under the thumb of society's incredible weight might leave you feeling light and, despite the bug bites and a few scrapes, maybe even slightly untouchable. Floating here and there and taking the express train out of town when things start feeling less than stellar, it's easy to start feeling that you'll never again have to deal with the same powers that once pinched your ear between thumb and index finger and informed you that regardless of what you thought, "this is how it's gonna be."

And then, perhaps when you least expect it, something like that does happen. You think you're a veteran hobo who can take himself from Seattle to Boston without spending any money or losing sleep over where the next buck is going to come from. Maybe you have just been pontificating to a newbie about the wonders of independent train travel, while hiding in a boxcar waiting to take off. Then you hear a crunching sound on the gravel and a light shines in your face. "Hey, come outta there!"

A few things could happen at this point. The bull with the light might tell you to skedaddle yourself right off of Union Pacific property with a stern warning that if you're ever caught on UP property again your next meal will be a free one but served behind bars on a metal tray. On the other hand, you may be given a ticket. Or you might get arrested on the spot. Word of caution: If you're arrested, *do not* pick a fight and try to escape. One: You'll probably lose. Two: If you do lose, which number one says you probably will, you could end up taking a beating. Three: What started out as a misdemeanor just got a little more serious.

Unless you've done something more serious than just sneak onto the train, most likely you'll be sent off or just given a ticket—which may sound like peanuts, but can be in the $500 range. However, if you had to partially dismantle a fence to get into the yard, or somehow managed to make a mess of things and cause a derailment, you could also be charged with damaging railroad property and can count on a ride in the back of a police car.

When you do end up in jail, theoretically you should have an arraignment within twenty-four hours—and up until that point you'll just have to get comfortable. At the arraignment, you'll get a chance to plead guilty or not guilty, and if you plead guilty you can get sentenced to a fine or time right then and there. If you plead not guilty, a hearing will be set—which you can pretty much guarantee won't be based on when it's convenient for you—when you'll have to appear before the judge again. In the best-case scenario, you'll put on a good show and the judge will let you go on your own recognizance until your court date. Assuming that happens, now you have some options. You can keep traveling and make it back for the date, you can decide to set up camp in the same area and wait for the date, or you can head on out with the hope that it'll never catch up with you. The latter has a high probability of coming back to haunt you later, and for that reason is not recommended.

> Even though you might be living the life and feeling the freedom and want to share it with everybody, resist the temptation to pull your hat off and wave to the people in the cars stopped at the railroad crossing as you fly past. Hobos commonly get ticketed or arrested when people who see them riding past on trains call it in to the police. Same goes for hitchhiking.

Getting arrested while on or near a freight train with a big pack on your back, however, does something to enhance the impression that you're a flight risk, so the judge may think if he lets you go you'll be on the first train out of town, and he may decide to hold you. If you can't make bail, you'll sit in jail until your hearing. So it's time to hope your Aunt Rita who lives four hours south feels generous enough to come and bail you out.

POSTING BAIL

If your aforementioned Aunt Rita won't make the drive to bail you out, or doesn't have the money, or she's out of town, or you don't have an Aunt Rita, you'll need to make bail some other way. You've probably heard about making bail all your life. Now you get to do it. Bail is a little like ransom. You give the court money that you can only get back when you show up at your hearing. Don't show up, you lose your money. For this reason bail is usually set at a price you can't afford to lose. Bail bondsmen generally set up shop where they're needed: across the street from where you are currently residing, and provide their contact info to the jail. Best to pick one of those instead of the guy your cellmate recommends, who he swears will give you a great deal.

Pick one, and then you'll have to fork over 10 to 15 percent of whatever your bail was set at. You can pay with cash, credit card, some kind of collateral (like the title to a car—you'd have to have said title on you for this to work), or they may agree to a payment plan (not the kind of people you want to skip payments on). The bondsman will then pay the court your bail in full, and when you do show up for court, he'll receive the bail back. And if you do use a bail bondsman, you do want to show up, because, in addition to the obvious reasons, if you don't, you'll need to be looking over your shoulder for the foreseeable future for some grizzly-looking guy employed as a bounty hunter. Better to show up.

YOU'RE LOST—OR MAYBE JUST TURNED AROUND

Standing at a crossroads or by the railroad tracks and not knowing which direction is which can be more than a little frustrating; you might hop a slow-moving train and then, only after it picks up speed and there's no option for getting off for the next ten hours, you discover you're going the wrong way. If you've been in contact with some people who promised you a few days work ten hours in the other direction, you can only hope they're the kind of people you can call and say you're on a freight train going in the wrong direction and you have no idea when you'll be there.

So how do you make sure you don't remain directionally challenged? Other than asking the person next to you (who may or may not have a better idea than you), there are a couple of ways.

Telling Direction by the Sun

To get the general gist, remember that the sun rises in the east and sets in the west. If it's morning or evening, this shouldn't be hard to determine, and then you can stick your arms out and with your left hand pointed west, you now know north is in front of you and south behind you. You'll feel pretty slick when you ask someone in town where the tracks are and he says just keep walking east and that's what you do, instead of slowly starting off in a vague series of directions and watching his face for clues as to whether you're hot or cold.

Telling Direction by Paper Clip and Water

If you're in the woods with little visibility beyond the tree canopy, take a paper clip or your sewing needle, rub it repeatedly on a dry piece of clothing—if you have something wool that's the best—and then place it on a leaf which you'll put in some still water. This can be a cup or pot with water in it, or a small still pool near a stream. A puddle will work perfectly. The paper clip will eventually turn to point north.

Telling Direction by the North Star

If it's nighttime and the stars are out, locate the North Star. If you're unsure of which dot in the sky that is, find the Big Dipper, imagine a line extending out from the handle about five times the handle's length. The star you find there is Polaris, the North Star. Back in business. (Of course, this isn't a foolproof method unless you're able to brush up on your constellations before you take off.)

Telling Direction by That Little Compass You've Had Since Second Grade

Assuming it still works after years spent knocking around in school desks and book bags, hold it out and follow the arrow.

DEALING WITH INJURIES

If you're working and staying in towns or cities, injuring yourself is not as dangerous because help—and professional help at that—is never too far way. If your problem is not life-threatening, in most cities you can usually find a free clinic (or at least a clinic where charges are figured on a sliding scale) that is geared to people without health insurance. These can be great places to go, for example, if you cut your hand on some rusty metal and need a tetanus shot. If you have health insurance, go wherever you know you'll be covered. For something more catastrophic, locate an emergency room and worry about the bills later.

When You Are Your Own Free Clinic

If you're not in a populated area but instead somewhere out in deserted land by the railroad tracks or just out in a national park camping, you might have to figure out how to patch yourself up by using your own two hands. Or you have the option of traveling with someone, in which case you can both put your heads together and think, "What would a doctor do?"

It can be rough out there, and you'll have plenty of opportunities to get injured. There are the obvious ones such as wrestling with 10,000 pounds of moving train car, to the smaller, and more mundane, scenarios, like walking down the tracks and twisting your ankle after losing your footing on the rock bedding or hooking your thumb on a fishhook while trying to bait it for the first time. These are common enough, so don't exacerbate the problem by being reckless and using your knife to pry things open with the point facing you. If you're in the midst of doing something and your little voice says something like, "This is pretty stupid, one slip and things are gonna get real ugly," stop what you're doing and look for another way.

It will be up to you to determine how dangerous an injury is to your well-being, and you'll have to use commons sense when it comes to the treatment. Get a few nicks on your legs while walking through the underbrush and you can be pretty sure you're going to live. Spraining your ankle might require you to take it easy for a few days but not necessitate an emergency room visit. Jumping from a train and breaking your arm because you landed funny is up there with injuries that warrant a trip to the hospital, as is walking through the woods and poking your eye with a tree branch (especially if you're not into the idea of having a glass eye).

Injuries are by no means a given, but for times when you are out there on your own, or even with a friend, and don't have immediate access to medical help, it's a good idea to have some rough first aid knowledge that can help to at least temporarily keep you mobile until you're able to get more professional help.

How to Stitch a Wound—but Not Replace an Eyeball

If you get a serious gash and it's clear you're going to need stitches, it would be nice—although not altogether an absolute prerequisite—if you had some basic sewing skills, such as the ability to reattach loose or missing shirt buttons. If you don't, after you've done this once or twice, you'll be sewing shirt buttons on in your sleep.

STITCHING YOURSELF

1. Wash the cut/wound really, really, well with water. The last thing you want is to sew in some dirt or debris that will fester in there, perhaps leading to gangrene and amputation of the limb in question.
2. Put some antiseptic—like iodine (or moonshine if you're in that neck of the woods)—on the cut.
3. Sterilize whatever you will be using as thread. You can either boil it (and in this case you could also put the needle in with it) or you could soak it in strong alcohol.
4. Take your smallest sewing needle and sterilize it either with your lighter or over a fire. Don't just wave it over the flame, but let it get engulfed for a minute and a half or so.

5. Thread your needle, and to better the story when you tell it later, put a stick or piece of bark in your mouth, and clamp down.
6. Convention is to insert the needle into your skin the same distance from the wound as the wound is deep. So stick the needle in, push it straight across to the other side of the wound, clamp down on the bark again, push it through the skin on the other side, pull it until the skin closes but don't make it super tight as it needs a little leeway to expand with swelling.
7. Once you're through, snip the thread and make a knot (this doesn't call for a figure-eight knot—any simple knot that won't pull through the hole will do). Repeat the process every ¼ inch or so.

After the cut has healed you can snip the stitches down the center, and pull them out from either side.

POISON IVY AND POISON OAK

While you're hiding out in bushes by the railroad tracks waiting for your train or hiking through the brush to get to your camp, you'll have plenty of opportunities to brush up against poison ivy or poison oak. If you're allergic and have run into them before, you probably know the drill. But if you've never suffered it or think you're immune, just be aware that for some people it can take more than a few exposures before you start having negative reactions in the form of blisters and rashes. Great stuff. So regardless of whether you're allergic or not, it's best to know how to identify the plants so you can steer clear.

Poison Ivy

Many learned the refrain, "Leaves of three, let it be," as children to recognize poison ivy. The leaves, in groups of three with one larger leaf and two smaller ones below and on either side of it, are often shiny due to the oil they secrete (which is what will cause a reaction when it comes into contact with your skin), and the leaves somewhat resemble a mittened hand—kind of smooth on one side of the leaf and the other side notched.

Since it's the oil that causes the problems, you don't have to touch the plant yourself—if your bag or pants rub against the plant the oil can then be transferred to you. Then, rather than scratch yourself, which will only aggravate the rash, kick and punch your bag for its traitorous behavior. The leaves are reddish in the spring, green in summer, and turn colors like other leaves in the fall.

Poison Oak

Another villainous plant out there pretending to be all innocuous and sweet is poison oak. It's similar to poison ivy, as they both have the three-leaf pattern, but this isn't a problem really as you don't need to tell them apart so much as you just need to stay away from them altogether. Poison oak, like poison ivy, will present itself differently depending on the season and your geographic location. As opposed to poison ivy which is red in the spring, poison oak is green, then a reddish green color somewhat similar to coral in the summer, and then a darker red in the fall.

I GOT IT, NOW WHAT DO I DO?

Once you've got it, you've got it. There is no cure other than time, so all you can do for yourself is to control the symptoms and discomfort the best that you can. Any anti-itch cream will help, hydrocortisone being one of the more popular. Another option is to make a paste from either oatmeal or baking soda that you place on the affected areas, which can both offer some relief and somewhat speed the drying/heal time. And when all else fails, some have even taken to covering the tiny blisters or rash from poison oak with duct tape, which will prevent your being able to scratch at it.

SNAKE BITES

If you're going to die on this adventure, it's more likely to happen from trying to hop a freight car (or even from eating a puffer fish at a Japanese restaurant for that matter) than from being bitten by a snake. But since it can happen, might as well be prepared.

So you're bit. You stare for a moment in mild shock that you were, in fact, just bitten by a snake and now, from what you've seen in the movies, you need to take a buck knife and cut an X over the cut and start sucking and spitting. Bring your mind back down to earth, and ask yourself the first question: Was it poisonous? Did you get a good look at the bastard? There are two main types of poisonous snakes in North America: the pit vipers (rattlesnakes, water moccasins, and copperheads) and coral snakes.

If you heard a rattle, that's a dead giveaway that it was a rattlesnake. The other pit vipers can be recognized by their wide triangular-shaped heads. Pit viper bites will leave one or two fang punctures, and will begin to really hurt in about five to ten minutes. Pit viper venom targets vascular tissue and red blood cells, and it may cause muscle twitches, chills, and excessive sweating.

Coral snake bites, on the other hand, sometimes do not leave visible fang marks. If you are deep in the southeastern or southwestern United States and you think the offender may have been the craziest looking snake you've seen in your life, with red, yellow, and black stripes, you just might have been the recipient of a coral snake bite. They release a neurotoxin which kicks in about ten to fourteen hours after being bitten and can cause paralysis.

> Coral snakes have some good imitators out there who want you to think they're super bad and deadly but actually aren't. One is the king snake, and the other has the fantastically innocuous name of milk snake. Get bit by one of these guys and avoid the unnecessary worry by remembering the helpful mnemonic: red on yellow, kill a fellow; red on black, friend of Jack. No sense trying to pull off an extreme yoga maneuver to suck venom out of your butt when there isn't any venom to suck. Much less asking a friend to do the honors.

Nonpoisonous snakes can bite you too, but they will not leave fang marks. Death by snake bite in the United States is quite rare, but it does occasionally happen, so unless you are sure that the snake was not poisonous, any snake bite should be taken seriously and treated immediately. If you are bitten, sit down, away from the snake, and try to stay calm. Keep the injured part to the same level or below the level of the heart. This avoids the fast expansion of the venom. Remove any restrictive clothing from the area, and all jewelry, and wrap the area tightly with a splint and bandage, similar to the way you would wrap a sprain. Then, as calmly and quickly as you can, get yourself to an ER. You may want to call ahead to warn them that you have been bitten by a snake so they can make sure and have the antivenom on hand when you get there.

If you're in the Southwest you may come across some Gila monsters, which not only look pretty dreadful, but can pack a solid poisonous punch for which there is no antidote available. The good news? Don't believe the hype. They are some of the slowest beasts west of the Mississippi, and you practically have to pin a Gila monster to the ground and stick your finger down its throat to get it to bite you.

STOMACH BUGS

If you get a stomach bug, make sure you keep yourself hydrated with clear liquids (not soda) taken frequently in small amounts. If you've got the runs multiple times a day, you're losing a lot of water, and dehydration is a constant risk. If you're going to be stuck without a bathroom for long periods of the day, taking some medication to stop yourself up is probably a good idea. But if you will have access, don't take anything and let it run its course. You'll get over it faster.

If you come down with a fever, take it as a signal from your body that you need to stop and take care of yourself. Boring but true: drink a lot of fluids. To keep the fever down you can take acetaminophen or ibuprofen, and once your temperature stays down without any meds, you're ready to start rolling again.

BLISTERS

You'll be on your feet a lot, and as such, you'll have to deal with blisters. It's easy to pass off blisters as wimpy injuries and no big deal, but blisters can cause fatal infections if not treated carefully. How do you deal with them? First take your knife—or a sewing needle if you have a little kit—and sterilize it over a fire or with a lighter. Then use your knife/needle to pop the blister at its bottom (not the top), so it will drain. Don't pull the skin off and leave the wound open, but rather leave it on for protection. Try to keep your feet dry and change your socks frequently until it is healed.

FROSTBITE

If you're going to be exposed to cold weather you need to avoid frostbite. It can happen on any part of the body, but it's particularly common on your fingers and toes. What makes frostbite tricky is that it can start to happen without your knowing it, since the main symptoms—numbness and pale color—are what you expect to feel when you're out in the cold.

What do you do if you get it? Start trying to warm up your frozen body parts (that's what they are) to bring them back up to normal temperature. You can do this either by holding it between your hands—unless it's on one of your hands, in which case a friend is necessary—or by putting it near a source of warm air or by immersing it in warm water. Don't rub or try to move around any toes or fingers that are frozen until they've thawed. Once they've warmed up, you can expect your skin to blister and peel. Let it do its thing and avoid messing with it, but make sure to keep your socks clean and dry. Keep an eye on it until it's completely healed.

CUTS

One of the fun things about completely changing your life and using a completely new set of tools to survive is discovering all new sorts of ways to injure yourself, and countless ways to cut yourself. For a fairly minor cut, clean it first, and then look for some yarrow (single-stemmed at around knee height, you'll know yarrow by its flat cluster of tiny white flowers). It grows everywhere, and is pretty amazing in its clotting ability—just press the flowers onto the cut for a moment. No yarrow? Use as clean a cloth as you've got and apply pressure. For the more severe cuts put pressure on the wound to slow the bleeding, and elevate the part of your body that you cut. If it's really bad and you can't stop the bleeding through pressure and elevation, fashion yourself a tourniquet above the injury, in effect isolating it from the rest of your body. It's probably time to get yourself to the ER at this point.

SPRAINS

It's fantastically easy to sprain your ankle or wrist. It can happen any time, hopping off a train, walking over rocks, climbing down to a river, what have you. Wrap the offending joint in an ACE bandage (no ACE bandage? If you have some gauze, you can use that in a pinch) and give it a rest. If you have the option to ice it—which you probably won't—you can do that initially, and after that heat will help. If you have no choice but to use it, try to brace it and trudge forth.

If you've done more than just sprain your ankle and have actually busted a bone, things are a little more involved. Particularly if the break is in a leg or foot, you can't just sit where you are until it heals hoping the birds drop food in your mouth, and moving around on it is gonna hurt like hell. You'll have to make a splint. You can make this from any stiff material you can find, including a tree branch. Tie it to the broken bit with clothing or rope. Whatever you use as a brace, it needs to span either side of the break or you're not helping yourself. Be super easy with it.

BURNS

If you burn yourself, don't put ice directly on the burned area (which won't be a problem if you don't have any ice). Instead, if you can, keep it cool by running water over it for ten to fifteen minutes or by submerging it in water that's around and pop some pain pills. If it's not a bad burn where your skin is blistering, your body will pretty much take care of it. Afterward, cover the area with a bandage until it has healed.

KEEP IN MIND

* In case of a broken bone that pierces the skin (open or compound fracture), you must apply pressure in order to control bleeding, but avoid pushing on any bone that is protruding through the skin.
* Don't ever try to straighten a broken, open-fractured limb; replace bone fragments; or return the limb to a natural position.
* Don't touch or try to clean the wound; just fasten a sterile or clean cloth securely in place over the wound and keep it in place with bandages or cloth strips.
* The splint must extend beyond the injured area to keep the limb from moving. Try to cover the joint below and the joint above the injury with the splint. Do not over-tighten, which can cut off circulation.
* Continue to check the area frequently for swelling, paleness, or numbness, and loosen the splint if needed.

SUNBURN AND THE HEAT

If you get a very bad sunburn, you can make a soothing ointment out of oak or hickory bark boiled in water. Apply this ointment to the burned area and cover it until it has healed, making sure to avoid further sun exposure.

If you're working outside in the heat, water is critical, but you can do yourself one favor more. That salt ring your clothes get after a hard-core workout is due to salt that was in your body and now isn't. Keep you salt levels up. When you have to work hard in the grueling heat, maintain your health by keeping an adequate water and salt intake. The rule of thumb is a quarter teaspoon of salt per quart of water. Drink enough to stay well hydrated—at least two quarts on a mild day, and more as you sweat more.

THINGS TO AVOID (AKA YOUR ENEMIES)

* Lice. Getting rid of them was the inspiration for the hobo term, to "boil up."
* Chiggers. You won't see them, but during the spring and summer they'll be hanging around in the grasses and weeds, waiting for someone just like you. Same as ticks, long pants can serve as a deterrent.
* Scorpions. Despite their deadly look, you'll probably be okay if stung. It'll hurt, burn, and swell a bit. If you start getting blurred vision, head to the doctor.
* Leeches. Slimy, nasty, vile, but essentially harmless.
* Parasitic worms. Purify your water and be picky if you visit the D-Mart.
* Deer ticks. Lyme disease can put a serious halt to your progress.
* Rabid raccoons, foxes, bats, or otters. You can generally assume these animals won't bother you; when you see them acting oddly brazen, rabies may be involved, so keep your distance.
* Brown recluse spider. Have you have ever seen pictures of what these little suckers can do?

* Black widow spider. Most bites are defensive when you inadvertently come into contact with them, and unfortunately, they don't all harbor the telltale hourglass on the belly.
* Copperhead snake. Kinda like the scorpion, their attacks are painful but generally not deadly.
* Rattlesnakes. They may not have ears, but contrary to the oft-told tale, they're not deaf.
* Water moccasins. Quite common on the coastal plains, a bite from them can cause gangrene. As you might expect, you'll find them in water.
* Grizzly bears. Too big to escape by climbing trees, grizzlies use a different method to protect themselves. They attack.
* Cougars. Territorial beasts, human attacks are pretty rare but there always seems to be the story about that one hiker . . .
* Alligators. You'll find these throughout the Southeast, and while they tend to be shy, they can also move at 30 mph in short bursts.

> ⚠ **REMEMBER:** Living your life on society's fringe can open you up to all sorts of nicks, scrapes, and traps, from getting picked up for trespassing on railroad property to sitting down on a brown recluse spider while bedding down in a barn. Always be aware of your surroundings, be resourceful, and keep your wits about you.

Did You Know Jack Kerouac Hoboed?

Jack Kerouac, born in 1922 and one of the forefathers of the Beat generation, traveled by freight and loved it. And wrote about it. He writes in *The Dharma Bums*, "The only alternative to sleeping out, hopping freights, and doing what I wanted, I saw in a vision would be to just sit with a hundred other patients in front of a nice television set in a madhouse, where we could be 'supervised.'" Perhaps more than others, his writings may be responsible for many a wide-eyed twenty-year-old heading out on the road with dreams of freedom and enlightenment, only to end up cursing his name while scrounging for vittles at the bottom of a dumpster.

And he did make it sound good. In stark contrast to the image of a simple hobo just looking to use his hands for a few hours in exchange for a meal, Kerouac tended to travel to and fro with stars in his eyes, plenty of booze in the belly, and dreams of starting a cultural revolution based on free love and Buddhism. Coming back into the United States from Mexico, Kerouac hitched a ride near the border with a trucker from the Midwest named Beaudry, and they proceeded (after a quick detour back into Mexico for a night of drinking) to travel to Tucson. When it came time for dinner, Beaudry complained about truck stop food, so Kerouac suggested that if he—Beaudry—bought the steaks, Kerouac would treat him to a true hobo feast by the side of the road. Which he did, starting a fire and cooking the steaks as cars and trucks flew past, and afterward cleaning out the pan with sand. Back in the truck Beaudry asked him, "Where'd you *learn* to do all these funny things?"

Kerouac brought out the poetry of free living while traveling across the country, and his books are filled with both poignant and adventurous moments. While other hobos had to toil away, ruining their bodies for pennies, Kerouac spent a summer on top of a mountain as a fire look-out and came down ready to spread the word.

But perhaps the approach to life he espoused is summed up best when, during one of many alcohol-fueled get-togethers, one of his companions, the poet Gary Snyder, eagerly interpreted Walt Whitman's line, "Cheer up slaves, and horrify foreign despots." This, Kerouac said, is simply another way of saying that someone with their vision sees "a world full of rucksack wanderers, Dharma Bums refusing to subscribe to the general demand they consume production and therefore have to work for the privilege of consuming . . . imprisoned in a system of work, produce, consume, work, produce, consume. I see a great rucksack revolution thousands or even millions of young Americans wandering around with rucksacks." So be it.

CONCLUSION

Remembering Where You've Been

"Later on he encountered yet another sort of men, those from whose ranks the tramps were recruited, men who were homeless and wandering, but still seeking work—seeking it in the harvest fields. Of these there was an army, the huge surplus labor army of society; called into being under the stern system of nature, to do the casual work of the world, the tasks which were transient and irregular, and yet which had to be done."

—UPTON SINCLAIR IN *THE JUNGLE* (1906)

By the time you pick yourself up off the floor of the last boxcar coming back into town and drop yourself to the ground, dust yourself off with your hat, and knock the stones out of your shoes, you will have become a veritable continental explorer. You are a person who can hop a freight train or hitch a ride and with just a bag on your back and a quarter in your pocket you can tour the country living life on your own terms. The only caveat: here and there you may have to spend a night (or two) in a ditch and may occasionally pick up a misdemeanor for trespassing.

You will have proven to yourself and to others that you can, despite all indications to the contrary, still live an independent and free life without sucking on a cultural airbag and feeding the meter in return. You will have set yourself free, and, for lack of a better description, weaned yourself from society's tit. Not something for the faint of heart.

In the process, you will have developed skills and abilities many have considered lost arts (and washing dishes without a dishwasher is just the tip of the iceberg when it comes to that). When traveling across the country for most entails "seeing" the country via two or three interstates at the most and having sampled the fast food at twenty-four different travel plazas, you will have traveled and seen the country in ways most never will, and by the look in your parents' eyes when you initially tell them your plans, in ways most never plan to. In an age in which litigation has come close to requiring you to wear a safety belt when riding the escalator at Macy's, you will have essentially ridden it while doing a handstand with a lollipop in your mouth (bear in mind that this was purely a metaphor, and in actuality, is probably even more dangerous than hopping a moving freight car in broad daylight—so don't try it to prove a point).

This could be one of the greatest periods in your life. It could also be one of the hardest, such that you live the rest of your days consoling yourself, in the face of any hardship, that at least it isn't as bad as the time you had to eat roast possum because you lost your pack and the only things you still had were your Swiss Army knife and a lighter. You may be one of those who goes on to hobo until you're old and gray, or you may take the ride as long as it suits you and then head back to a job and family. Alternatively, you may become an intermittent hobo—hooking up with old buddies and taking to the rails for a few weeks or a month each year. As said in the beginning, there are no rules and regulations as to how you should approach any of this. The whole idea is to shed some constraints and see what comes of it.

You will meet characters. Some of them you will become friends with and relish the chance to meet again. Others you will do your very best to forget, considering yourself lucky that they chose the wrong fish sandwich at the last dumpster you shared and had to bow out of the next day's journey. You'll try to remind yourself to write a postcard to the guy in Wichita who stopped and gave you a ride to the next exit even though it was forty minutes out of his way and you could tell by his quiet smile he was putting your last shower about a week prior, at best. You'll want to tattoo a sign on the back of your hand telling you to never, ever, share a boxcar with a guy who asks you what your sign is before asking your name.

There's one suggestion you've probably heard all your life but never done it, so this time do it: Write it down. While you're out there, it's easy to see and feel things that make you think, "I will never forget this." But then you will. Maybe not immediately, and maybe not in six months, but over the course of a few years, experiences that at the moment seemed as crisp and tangible as the railroad spike you held in your hand and used to "spike" the boxcar's door will slowly fade and change. One day you'll try to recall it, but it will be such a blurry mess that you won't remember whether it happened to you or if it was just a story someone else told you, and you'll vaguely remember something having to do with a railroad spike. Don't let it happen. Write it down. Keep a travelogue. Use it. Make a point of setting aside some time each day to make a few notes that can later serve as mental signposts that can guide you back to the moment and push the fog away. You'll be kicking yourself in the head ten, fifteen, or twenty years later when you're sitting around a table trading stories with friends and you excitedly start to relay a tale and then have to say, "Wait, damn . . . I can't remember what he said." And that was probably the punch line. Remember to put it down.

Don't get sucked into writing everything in extreme detail or you'll burn yourself out within a few days and never go back to doing it because it was such a pain in the ass. Make it easy, not obsessive. Just enough so you'll be able to jog your memory later, at which point you can flesh it out and bring it to life—rather than when you're trying to write by firelight and the mosquitoes are whining in your ear.

But it will serve more than just you and your memories if you keep some sort of journal as you go. It will also help you help others down the road. You may not ever head in a particular direction again, but others will, and when you bump into them, either in a jungle or at a greasy spoon or sitting across from them in a gondola, and they ask where to catch out in San Francisco and if you had a favorite flop house in the Tenderloin, you might just have the answer—if you remembered to write it down.

And should you continue your own rambling lifestyle, your travelogue can serve you as well. Filled with points of interest, places to stay, people to look up who helped you out, potential friends, places to work, places to get the best blueberry pancakes west or east of the Mississippi, places to catch out from, places not to catch out from, and the place you got arrested and later had to walk six miles to link back up with the railroad outside of "that guy's" jurisdiction, you'll rely on this written history to bring your hobo experience back to life in an instant.

Furthermore, things that seemed incredibly mundane to you at the time and that you just took for granted can blow someone else's mind if they've never heard or seen such a thing before. Don't waste this opportunity. Write it down. You'll be glad you did.

APPENDIX A

Tips for the Modern-Day Hobo

While the idea of taking your life on the road may seem like exactly the thing you want to do, hopping a freight train might seem ludicrous and not even close to what you have in mind. Rather, you believe in the spirit of what those original hobos stood for, but just as you have no intention of going out back and swinging a chicken by its neck because that's how they "used to do it," you also have no intention of putting on dark clothes so you can sneak around a train yard at night without having a confrontation with the bulls that could lead either to jail or just a little unpleasant shoving around along with a ticket.

You will be a modern-day version of that nineteenth-century hobo, traveling the country and making enough money to live on while having no fixed address. For you, this could be a six-month experiment after which you'll go back to your "normal" life, or it could be a lifelong endeavor. Instead of hopping freight trains and working labor jobs that require you to continue to be physically able and that eventually lead you to the assessment that you're just too old to be doing this anymore, you might have the option to live this way indefinitely. If the only thing you need to maintain an income is a working laptop with an Internet connection, the world is ready for you. You don't even really need a phone anymore.

When looking for places to stay for the night, you can still camp, but you'll need to be more careful with your gear. If you can afford it, a number of companies make ruggedized laptops, often with labels having some claim to being military ready. One might assume that if they can handle cruising over off-road terrain in a Humvee, they may be able to handle much of what you're going to put it through, although you would probably still want to avoid leaving it in a puddle or dropping it on a rock.

SETTING UP WIRELESS

There are many ways to keep an Internet connection while traveling. Cafés offering free wireless Internet can be found in almost any town, and if the ones you're near don't, or you're not in a town, you can use your cell phone as a wireless modem. If you have a smartphone and you have reception, you're already on the Internet. The Internet may be the biggest advantage you have over the hobos of old (comfortable cars and buses notwithstanding). You can have a virtual presence anywhere in the world while connected, and so can set up jobs and receive money without having to move.

Different Ways to Achieve an Internet Connection

1. Use a smartphone.
2. Use a laptop using your cell phone as a modem.
3. Find free WiFi hot spots in public places.
4. If you're traveling in an RV and plan to park for extended periods, purchase satellite Internet.

BILLS AND PAYPAL

Set up bill pay. If you have credit cards and a cell phone, have these bills directly paid from your account each month without having to remember, find a stamp, or even be awake. If you happen to be somewhere "out there" and your phone gets shut off, it might be some time before you're able to get to a place where you can have it turned back on.

If you don't have one already, get a PayPal account. This is one of the easiest ways to send and receive money. People can pay you with PayPal and the money will be deposited directly into your bank account, and if you have an account with one of the larger banks and an ATM, that can translate into actual cash fairly quickly.

SEND AND RECEIVE ACTUAL MAIL

As archaic as it may seem, there are times when you may need to receive actual, physical mail. How do you do this when you're always on the move and have no physical address someone can send something to? One easy way is to pull out the map and locate a small town or city you'll be passing through in a week's time. Find the number for the post office and call and tell them when you'll be coming through, and see if they will accept mail addressed to you. Small towns are better, as their post office is usually more accommodating than those of big cities, which have a few more things to concern themselves with besides caring for a letter from some transient passing through. And that's if you can even get them on the phone to begin with.

One thing to be slightly wary of when sending mail is that you have no return address, and if, for any reason, the mail turns out to be undeliverable, it will end up in the bottom of a bin somewhere, never to be heard from again.

SOME WAYS TO MAKE MONEY ONLINE

Blog

Try to keep a running journal of your travels and post it to your blog. Doesn't matter if no one reads it at first, but if you can keep it interesting, and even post some videos, you may eventually get a following. How does this help? People will start to take note, and you may be able to start making some money by hosting ads on your blog.

Though not immediate, keeping a running log of your travels also puts you in a good place to eventually put out a book. All the more reason to take pictures along the way and write a daily journal to keep things fresh in your mind. What may seem uninteresting now may seem incredibly interesting to someone else. Don't censor yourself.

How to Set Up a Blog

You don't need to be able to code html or use Dreamweaver to start a blog, or need any money. There are several sites you can find by a simple search that will host your blog. You just have to come up with a name and then fill in the blanks with whatever it is you want to write. Super easy.

One way you may be able to spontaneously become a breakout star is to travel with a video camera and post your videos. It may seem ridiculous at first, but you're going to come across some random and wild things over the course of your journeys, and if you happen to catch a particularly ridiculous moment on camera, post it and who knows? It might turn viral and the next time you go online you'll discover your video has had a million hits and people are scrambling to get a hold of you. Wouldn't bank on it, but wouldn't be too bad if it happened, either.

Write Short Article for Sites

They usually pay a pittance, but if you can write 500 words on how to paint a room or change a bike chain, you can pump a number of these out and get cash to keep you going.

Get Rich Quick Schemes

If you start looking on the Internet for businesses you can run online, you'll run into a bazillion promising wealth beyond what you've ever dreamed, and all from the comfort of wherever you happen to be. In fact, some will promise that you don't have to do anything and you'll be earning money. Do yourself a favor and forget about it. They're all designed to suck you of your last dollars with little chance you'll ever make any money yourself. It's probably better to keep visiting the D-Mart than try your hand at any of these.

APPENDIX B

The Hobo Cookbook

Hobos gotta eat, you know. Here are some essential tips to eating sans kitchen—and sans money, for that matter.

COFFEE

For some there's no getting up in the morning without coffee, so we'll start here. Don't let the fact that you're a simple hobo without a programmable auto-drip coffeemaker stand in your way. Bring on the Cowboy Coffee. Take coarse-ground coffee and put it in a pot with water. Bring it to a boil, then let it sit long enough that all the grounds sink to the bottom. Talk about easy. For an even more authentic experience, strain the coffee through a clean sock to remove all the gritty grains. This can have the effect of turning the stomach of any guest you might have, but a quick demonstration that the sock is clean and not one you just hiked all day in should set them straight.

PINE NEEDLE TEA

If coffee isn't your thing, but you want something to warm you up and get you going on those chilly mornings, try brewing up a pot of Pine Needle Tea. Since evergreens never lose their needles, the main ingredient is available all year long. And besides getting you going in the morning, this tea will also help boost your immune system and fight off colds.

PINE NEEDLE TEA

Several clusters of pine needles

1 quart boiling water

Lemon juice from 1 lemon

Maple syrup to taste

1. Using scissors, snip needles into small pieces.
2. Pour boiling water over needles. Add lemon juice.
3. Cover and let steep 5 minutes.
4. Sweeten to taste and enjoy.

BANNOCK BREAD

This recipe was brought over to the United States by Scottish fur traders in the early 1800s. It can be pan-fried or baked on a stick, as described below. Its recipe is super flexible; basically consisting of flour, baking soda, water, and some oil, plus whatever else you happen to have to throw in.

BASIC BANNOCK BREAD

1 cup flour

1 teaspoon baking powder

¼ teaspoon salt

1½ tablespoons oil

About ½ cup cold water (or enough to make the dough thoroughly wet, but not so wet that it is sticky)

Mix all of the above in something other than the pan in which you mean to cook it (if you only have one bowl or pan, consider making it on a stick described below). It should be a thick, pasty consistency. Below are some directions, but keep in mind this is one meal where you can really wing it.

BANNOCK-IN-A-PAN

1. Put the pan on the heat and toss in a generous amount of whatever oil you've got on hand.
2. To make one "loaf," spread the dough out in the pan evenly; it should be anywhere from ¼ to ½ inch thick.
3. Cook away. Think of it as a giant pancake that you don't have to flip.
4. Consider it done when it's firm on top.

BANNOCK-ON-A-STICK

1. Get the right stick for the job. Look for a green stick (or any stick that won't quickly turn into firewood) approximately 1–2 inches thick and long enough to comfortably hold over the fire.
2. You'll need to remove the bark to expose a smooth surface to wrap the bread around while cooking it.
3. Preheat the far end of the stick above the fire until it is hot, then wrap the bannock dough about ½ inch thick around the stick.
4. Hold the bannock above the fire, turning it as it cooks, and trying not to char any of the sides. The perfect height for cooking the bannock is where you can hold your hand above the fire for about 10–15 seconds.

BAKED POTATOES

These are super easy. Just plunk them in the coals and wait a half hour or so till they are soft. Make sure to poke a few holes in the skin to allow steam to escape, or you could end up surprising yourself with an exploding hot potato.

CORN ON THE COB

Also simple. Ideally, you would soak the corn in water for a half hour to an hour to keep them from burning, but depending on conditions this may or may not be possible. If you don't have the water available, just keep an eye on 'em. Place the whole ear (unhusked) on the coals. The husks will keep the moisture in and the ash out as the corn steams away. Depending on the heat of your fire, this could take anywhere from ten minutes to an hour, and make sure you turn here and there. Good idea to check on it after ten minutes or so just to see what's going on. Done when tender. Didn't come out so great the first time? You're in luck. What else do you have to do other than practice? Try another one.

NETTLE SOUP

Nettles are some of the most nutritious vegetables on the planet, and you probably never would have guessed it growing up, as you were always being warned to avoid them. Sure enough, be careful not to touch them with your bare hands before cooking them. The only required ingredients for the soup are the nettles, the water, and salt to taste. Everything else is optional. With whatever you have on hand, this could turn into a mulligan, easy.

NETTLE SOUP

Around 1 pound nettles. Give them a quick wash and chop/tear them up.

About 1 quart of water

Some salt

1 onion chopped and fried in a bit of oil until it's soft (optional)

A few cloves of garlic, just peel them and crush them with the flat side of your knife (optional)

1–2 potatoes, chopped (optional)

1 carrot, chopped (optional)

Some rice or other grain (optional)

Boil this business until everything is tender.

DANDELION SALAD

Really, this is actually quite good. Make a dressing out of a lime or lemon squeezed over the greens with a little oil and garlic. Change-up the salad however you want. Add some dried fruit, nuts, leftover quinoa, some seeds you stole from a squirrel, anything at all. You don't even have to use dandelions if there are none around; you can substitute any edible greens you have on hand (just don't call it a dandelion salad).

BE CAUTIOUS WHEN FORAGING

If you're interested in foraging while you travel, you should find out which wild plants are poisonous, and which ones might be confused with an edible plant is important. It is recommended that you learn the poisonous ones first and then feel free to experiment with the ones that you know are edible.

When gathering wild greens, there are a few plants to be aware of. Buttercups hide amongst the leaves of chickweed and dandelion and are sometimes picked with them. Members of this family contain glycosides that have caused irritations among livestock. Spurges are also common in gardens and lawns. They produce a milky sap that can also be irritating. Pokeweed leaves, when eaten raw, will make you throw up, even though they are edible when cooked. Milkweed is another plant that is edible when cooked but toxic raw.

HOW TO COOK FISH

Most fish you will catch will be the size that is best cooked whole. Anything over ten pounds can be filleted or boned, but smaller fish are not worth the trouble. Fish is quite versatile and can be grilled, fried, boiled, baked, steamed, or poached. If you want to be extra fancy, you can nail it open on a plank, which you then prop up next to the fire to cook by reflected heat for ten to twenty minutes. No matter which method of cooking you choose, you should cook the fish until the flesh is opaque and flaky, but not so long that it gets dry. Garnishes that almost always make fresh fish taste out of this world are lemon and/or butter. Garlic, herbs, and onion never hurt either. Use what you have to make your dinner special.

COOKING YOUR FOOD

How you cook largely depends on your source of heat. Here are a few common methods.

Cooking over a Fire Pit

If you made a fire pit as described earlier, you might be looking at this magnificent survival feat you pulled off and then wonder how you're ever going to cook over it. One way is to just set a pot on the coal. You can also wrap your food in tinfoil, and then lay it on the edge of the fire. Or you can make a suspension system for hanging your food over the fire. Find a Y-shaped stick, or something approaching that. Drive it into the ground near the fire. Take another stick and with one end supported in the nook of the Y-shaped stick, put the other end on the ground beside the fire. Hang your pot.

Cooking with a Hobo Stove

Another useful cooking method that uses very little fuel and is easy to manage is the hobo stove. Wonder who came up with that? There are any number of ways to make one of these, and if you're gonna be in one place for a while, it will save your fuel for emergencies. If you're a carpenter and have some tools packed, you should be all set for this. If not, you can make do with a Leatherman or other multipurpose tool.

What you will need is a large empty food can or coffee can, and if you have a small soup-sized can you can use that as a pot. Turn the can upside down so the open end is facing the ground. Now, cut a rectangular opening in the bottom (actually now the top) of the can, making something akin to a mini garage door. This is where you'll insert the tinder. Next cut another hole near the top (which is actually now the bottom of the can) to serve as a flue to let the smoke escape. The bottom of the can is your cooking surface, on which you can place a soup can or what have you. This stove works great even in quite exposed and windy conditions.

An alternative version of the hobo stove is to use a larger can; an unused paint can is perfect. Cut the bottom off, insert at least two small rods through the can (anything you can find that won't burn), and then you can lower a small pot down from the top of the can and let it sit on the rods, above the heat.

QUICK TECHNIQUE

Once you get your fire going and you've got some good coals, you need to prepare it for cooking. First, spread the coals out in a grade so that there is a region with lots of heat and another region with less heat. This will give you some control over the cooking speed as needed.

If you're using a grill, you need to prop it about four to twelve inches above the coals. A good way to find the right height is to hold your hand above the coals. The right height for the grill is four inches below the spot where you can hold your hand still for no more than a second or two.

If you're tire-tramping it (i.e., have your own vehicle) and camping, a cast iron Dutch oven may be your best friend when it comes to dinnertime. The most useful style of Dutch oven for campfire cooking has a concave lid with a rim around its edge, allowing you to put a layer of hot coals above the interior. If you can find a Dutch oven with a lid that doubles as a skillet, all the better. The Dutch oven serves as a soup pot, an oven, and a frying pan all in one, and if you take care to maintain its seasoning (*never* wash it with soap), its nonstick surface will make your life quite easy.

When it comes to actual cooking, there are some methods you can try other than just using pots. It just so happens there is such a thing as a "hobo meal," otherwise known as cooking your dinner in a foil packet. As you might expect, when you're trying to travel light, a roll of tinfoil is a whole lot lighter than a pan.

> Heavy-duty foil works way better than regular, thin foil, since it won't snag or tear on the coals as easily. And if you don't have any foil at all, you can gamble a bit by substituting some damp newspaper or paper napkins; it's not so ideal but can work in a pinch—which is what you'll be learning a lot of on your travels: making things work in a pinch.

There are two main approaches to the hobo meal, flat and tented. Each is a bit better suited for certain kinds of food; flat for foods you're trying to roast, and tented for foods you're more interested in steaming like that broccoli someone gave you in the grocery store parking lot when she saw your pack and face and figured you deserved a hand.

SETTING UP YOUR HOBO MEAL

1. For both types of packets, the method of wrapping is simple. First, tear off a piece of heavy-duty foil that is more than twice the length of the food you are preparing. You should overestimate here, as underestimating could leave you with an ashy dinner.
2. Fold the foil ends together over the food and then fold the edge over itself a few times, making an airtight seal. If you are making

the flat packet, you should fold the foil down until it is very close to the top surface of the food and then flatten it by pressing lightly. If you are aiming for the tented packet, leave some air space above the food.

3. Now fold in the ends. Make sure you can fold each end in at least twice, in order to make an airtight seal again.
4. Then, holding the packet by the ends, place it in the coals and wait until you think the food is done, and then see if it is.

For steaming packet meals, you'll get a softer heat when you combine the foil and newspaper methods. First, make your foil packet as described above, then wrap the packet in wet newspaper and then another layer of foil. This will keep your food from charring at the edges where it's closest to the coals. When you open your foil or newspaper packet, be careful of the steam trapped inside—don't open it near your face.

The main consideration when cooking packet meals is the cooking time of the contents. It is important that all the ingredients that you toss into the packet will cook in approximately the same amount of time. The cooking time for a food depends on its density. For instance, carrots and potatoes take longer to cook than onions and celery. Meat falls somewhere in between. That doesn't mean that you can't put carrots, potatoes, onions, celery, and steak in a packet together, it just means that you have to cut the chunks that you include such that they will cook in the right span of time. Larger chunks take longer to cook than smaller chunks. So, you'd include small slices of carrots and potatoes, a larger thickness of steak, and even larger chunks of onion and celery. This may sound confusing, but just go with your gut and you'll get the hang of it in no time.

APPENDIX C

Essential MacGyver Skills

Depending on whether you stay in urban areas or go into the wild, you'll need to have some skills at your side.

KNOTS

If you skipped the whole Boy Scouts thing as a kid and haven't spent much time in the merchant marines, tying good knots may not be among your stronger suits. But a lot of things can go wrong for the lack of a good knot, so it behooves you to know a few. You might be thinking you can tie your shoes, and that's as good a knot as any and it'll serve you in every situation. It is a good knot, but not for every situation. Where might you need some knots?

WHERE KNOTS GO

* Hanging a drying line for some laundry between some trees or just on someone's back porch.
* Hanging your bear bag at the campsite.
* Tying extra items to your pack.
* Tying your pack and a few other things to the roof of a car because you just got a ride from someone with a two-seater and they say, "You're welcome to a ride if it can fit."
* You lose some of your tent stakes and have to tie your tent down.
* Tying pieces of firewood together to make it easier to schlep back to camp.

A lot of things can go wrong for lack of a good knot. The basic deal about knowing a good knot is knowing which one to apply in a specific situation. Making a knot is not all that difficult, most of us have, at some point in our lives, wrapped and twisted and tucked rope around this way and that way until it seemed to hold well enough. But there are two problems with this. One, your use of rope is not going to be that efficient, and since you're probably never sure when enough is enough you'll either just use more or you actually won't use enough and whatever it was that you meant to tie won't stay tied very long. The second problem lies in untying it. After it's strained under a load, it may have been pulled too tight, and undoing it is no longer possible. With this method there's usually only one solution, which is to cut it. And after a dozen or so such knots along your journey, what started out as a single fifty-foot piece of rope will eventually turn into a dozen shorter pieces that may not work for what you need and will just be a pain to keep track of. A knot is good if it holds where it's supposed to hold and can easily be undone regardless of the load it's holding or whether the rope has become wet.

Simple solution? Learn a few good ones. And practice before you need one. Knowing the steps in your head can be pretty different from actually standing there with some rope in your hand while a storm brews and you need to tie your tent down. If you don't have any rope yet, you can practice with anything. A shoelace will do.

SOME KNOT TERMS TO KNOW

* **Standing end:** This is the end of the rope that's not involved in the knot. If you were to wrap a rope around your friend's waist and then slowly lower him over a cliff (not recommended), the end of the rope you have in your hand is the standing end.
* **Bight:** Any curved section between the two ends of the rope.
* **Loop:** Where a rope is crossed over itself to form, well, a loop, this is a loop.

* **Bitter end:** The usually rather short end of rope that is tied off. This is the inspiration for the saying, "hanging on to the bitter end." It's not a good thing.
* **Working end:** This is the end of the rope you're using to make the knot.

Bowline

One of the most popular knots, often referred to as the "king of knots." It normally does not slip and can be untied wet or even when tension has been applied. Great for tying a length of rope to a tree. The little story used to teach the tying of it goes: "the rabbit comes out of the hole, goes around the tree, and goes back into the hole."

HOW TO TIE A BOWLINE

1. Make a crossing turn.

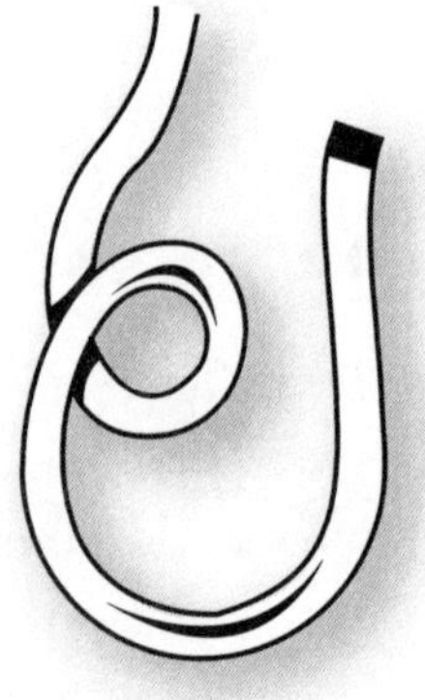

2. Bring the working end back up through the loop. And then bring it under the standing part of the rope.

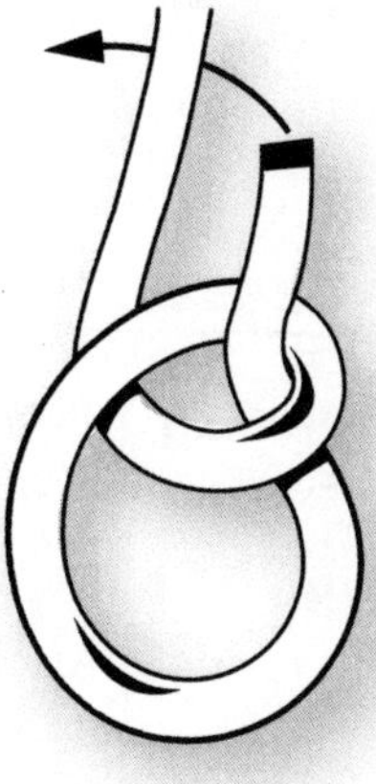

3. And now bring it back down through the small loop.

4. Pull it tight.

Sheet Bend

This is the knot to use when you have two lengths of rope of the same diameter, and neither is long enough by itself. Use it to combine them, the way a prisoner ties a whole bunch of bed sheets together in a line to escape from a tower.

HOW TO TIE A SHEET BEND

1. Make a loop in rope A, with the working part over the standing part. Then bring the working end of rope B up through the loop in rope A.

2. Now bring B's working end under A's standing part.

3. Finally bring B's working end down through the loop in rope A and pull tight.

To make what's sometimes called a "stopper knot," where you don't want the bitter end to pull through, make a figure-eight knot.

Figure-Eight Knot

The Figure-Eight Knot is frequently used as a basis for other knots. It's easy to untie and is not damaging to rope fibers. Because the Figure-Eight Knot has a distinctive "figure eight" look, it's easy to check to make sure it's tied correctly.

HOW TO MAKE A FIGURE-EIGHT KNOT

1. Make a loop over the standing part. Then bring the working end under the standing part.

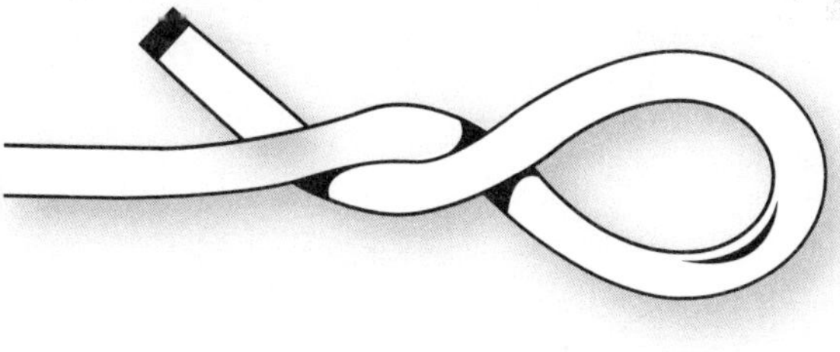

2. Now bring it over the first loop you made.

3. And bring it down through the loop and tighten. At this point you can see where the knot got its name.

Clove Hitch

This hitch ties quickly, but should not be considered a permanent connection or be used for safety or heavy loads. It could prove useful when you are collecting firewood.

HOW TO TIE A CLOVE HITCH

1. Pass the running end around the object, cross over the standing part, and then pass the running end around the object again; then tuck it under the crossing.

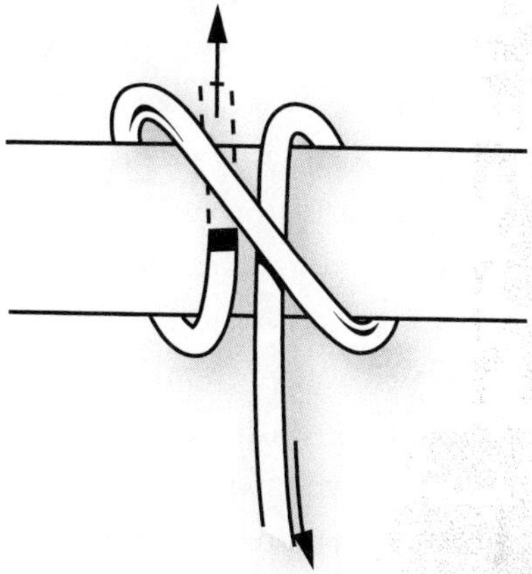

2. Tighten the knot around the object.

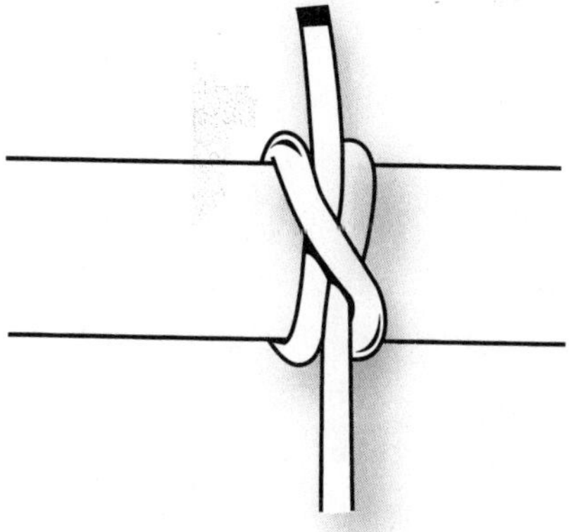

HOW TO WATERPROOF YOUR MATCHES

Everyone's lighter dies at some point, and almost without exception you only realize it's dead when you're trying to use it. Another scenario is where you might be digging around to find your lighter to make a fire and you drop it in the snow; with its wet flint it'll be out of commission for a while. And you don't even have to drop it. Pull out your lighter in the rain and a few random drops can ruin your dinner, or whatever else it was you were hoping to set on fire. For these times, with the exception of some flint and steel, nothing beats a waterproof match. You can find a number of different brands advertising themselves as "waterproof" or "windproof."

True enough, these will cost you a little extra, some of them are better than others, and if the only place in town is a nickel-and-dime shop with long-faded mannequins and products that time has forgotten in the their cloudy display cases, chances are they're not going to be carrying the latest and greatest in waterproof matches. But you probably will be able to find some basic household items in there, and turpentine and candles, even if they were put on the shelf thirty years ago, will still do the trick you're looking for. You're about to make your own waterproof matches. There are several ways to do this.

Turpentine

Turpentine is probably the easiest method of waterproofing matches. Fill a small dish—a shot glass is perfect—with turpentine (you don't need much, just enough that you can submerge the head of a match plus an eighth of an inch or so of the stick). Then put in your matchsticks and let them sit for five minutes. When they're done, take them out and let them dry out on a piece of cardboard or newspaper. After twenty minutes you're good to go. The cool thing about using turpentine rather than wax is that you won't have to spend any time trying to scrape the wax off the match head, which if it's raining can lead to the unfortunate result that by the time you've scraped the wax off, the head has gotten soaked.

> Can't find anywhere to strike matches? You should have a container with a lid where you keep your matches. Glue a small piece of fine sandpaper to the underside of the lid. Kerpow. Instant strike.

Candle Wax

Light a candle, and melt enough wax that you can, as with the turpentine, submerge the match head and a bit of the stick as well. Once coated, pull out the match, let it semi-harden, and while it is still malleable pinch the wax around the match head to form a neat and tight seal.

THREE THINGS ABOUT THIS METHOD

* If you have a large candle that makes for a nice pond of melted wax, that's great.
* Blow out the candle before submerging the match or you run the risk of igniting your matches well before showtime.
* When the time comes to light one of these, you'll need to scrape off the wax with your fingernail until you've exposed enough surface area on the match head to strike and light.

Nail Polish

You can either dip the matches into the bottle of nail polish, or use the brush. Either way, coat the match and some of the stick and let it dry. You can hang them over the edge of the counter, table, or anything that keeps the match head fully exposed. After it's dried, apply another coat and let it dry. Done.

SEWING

Since you're not changing pants everyday but wearing the same ones over and over, and over, they're going to get a lot of wear and tear, whether it's from catching your clothes on a chain-link fence as you crawl through a small opening or just the inevitable hole in the armpit, you don't want to be coming apart at the seams a few months into your trip so that when you stroll into town people start wondering if you're a hermit who's come down from the mountain after several years just to see if the world was still there.

To combat this—and the need to come up with sudden pockets of cash for new clothes every time you experience a breakdown—every hobo should know how to mend their own clothes. Most people probably wouldn't consider sewing much of a MacGyver skill, but if you don't currently have any sewing skills, you might—particularly when you save yourself a trip to the ER by employing them for stitching up your own wounds (or some other trusting soul's).

CONTENTS OF A BASIC SEWING KIT

* Thick thread.
* Some thinner thread.
* A few needles (when you only have one and drop it into the underbrush, well, there's a reason for the saying, "like looking

for a needle in a haystack"). Plus, thinner needles are easier to get through most material, but if the material is really tough—like leather—a thicker needle will help. Always carry a few.

* Keep a thimble in there; you'll fall in love with it if you have to push a needle through tough material.
* Small pair of scissors (though you might already have a pair on your multiuse knife).

Seam Rips

Seam rips are tears where the thread holding two sections of fabric together has ripped, rather than the fabric itself. These are some of the easiest problems to fix, since all you're doing is just replacing—or reinforcing—the thread. These kinds of fixes don't alter the shape of whatever it is you're fixing. When faced with such a predicament you could just have at it and thread a needle with some thread, tie a knot, and then do a whole lot of back and forth from side to side, tie another knot, and then snip it. Or, for a more lasting and sturdy repair try the following.

LONG-LASTING SEWING REPAIR, THE "BACKSTITCH"

1. Thread a needle with a length of the thinner thread that is at least 4 times as long as the rip, or 1½ fcct, whichever is longer.
2. Tic the ends off together in a knot, as close to the ends of the thread as possible, leaving a double-thickness of thread attached to the needle.
3. Hold the seam together and, starting behind the fabric, pull the thread toward you through both thicknesses of fabric until the knot catches.

4. You should start the sewing about 1 inch above where the seam actually comes apart. Make sure to pull the thread tight with each stitch, to avoid tangles.
5. About ¼ inch from where the thread is coming through the fabric, put the needle back through the fabric, this time drawing the thread away from you.
6. To make the next stitch, backtrack to the middle of the stitch that you just made, and bring the needle toward you through both thicknesses of fabric. Again, take this stitch back through the fabric in about ¼ inch. Repeat the process. You should be getting a good idea at this point of the pattern you're making.
7. Continue this until you're about 1 inch past where the seam had broken, then put the needle back through the fabric, slide the needle under the last stitch that you made, make a double knot, and snip the thread. Bang. You nailed it. Good as new.

Button Falls Off

This problem is just about as easy as the seam mending. You will need about twelve to eighteen inches of your thick thread, threaded through the eye of the needle and knotted together at the ends as described in the seam bit above. Bring the thread up initially where you want the button to go (the original placement of the button is usually pretty easy to determine if you look hard enough), from behind the fabric. Pull till the knot catches. Make a few small stitches in the fabric to secure the end, then put the needle up through the fabric again where the button will go and thread the needle through one of the holes in the button. Bring the thread down again through the opposite hole in the button and back down through the fabric, making a stitch across the button. Repeat this stitch once or twice, then move to the other two holes, making a few stitches forming an X across the center of the button. You should leave a little bit of slack in the stitches so that the button's final placement isn't tight against its backing fabric but instead a bit loose, allowing easy manipulation.

Fabric Rip

There are two options for this fix. You can either treat the rip like a new seam and sew it up from behind like you would a seam rip, or you can treat it like a hole, in which case you'd patch it as described below. Your call. Either way, the remedy will usually be noticeable, so if it's a work shirt, no biggie; if it's your dress shirt you were planning to wear out to the club, well—just hope it's dark.

Hole

Holes need to be patched with new fabric. You should take care to fold the edges of the patch under as you go so that the loose threads do not escape and look ratty. You can use a zigzag stitch or a whipstitch to attach the patch to the fabric.

You can also find iron-on patches at a lot of stores. While they're not as strong as a patch you've sewn on, you can make them as strong by throwing in some stitching around the edges. Granted, even if you did toss an iron into your pack before you left, it's going to require electricity to get hot. Might not be so easy to come by in a boxcar.

Zipper Gets Off Track

There may be nothing more annoying than going to zip up your jacket and the zipper gets off track (though having the same problem with a zip-up sleeping bag might come in at a close second).

The feasibility of fixing the zipper depends on the problem. If some of the teeth are missing, this is gonna be a little like replacing the engine in the car that you no longer have, so in that respect it will be easier. But it will involve carefully removing the entire zipper and replacing it. So if it's your fly, wear a long shirt or keep your jacket closed while you shop around for a new one.

If none of the teeth are missing, but the zipper has just become misaligned, this you can fix out in the field. You're going to remove the little metal bumper at the closed end of the zipper, realign the teeth, and then create a new bumper; minor surgery.

THE ZIPPER REUNITED

1. The removal of the metal bumper will not be easy, so be prepared to struggle with it, and if you haven't already, congratulate yourself on bringing a multiuse tool that has a small pair of pliers included. What is the metal bumper? It's the little metal piece at the bottom of the zipper that doesn't look like the other teeth and keeps the zipper from falling off when you unzip it.
2. With the bumper removed, slowly zip the zipper closed, making sure that all the teeth fit together. Don't force it. If it closes, move on to the next step. If not, bang it with a rock in retaliation until it's unrecognizable and then commend yourself for at least trying.
3. If the zipper does close nicely, up and down, it's time to sew on a new bumper. "But wait!" you say, "You didn't mention I needed a new bumper!" You don't. You're going to mimic one with your thick thread, sewing anywhere from five to ten stitches where the bumper had been and then finally tying off the thread on the backside of the fabric. If your zipper falls off your thread "bumper," then you didn't make it big enough.

Notes

Resources

WEBSITES WITH HOBO INFORMATION/ STORIES/ARTICLES

Fred's Website—*www.northbankfred.com*
A really great resource for freight-hopping stories and articles. Also, check out its companion site:

Black Butte Center for Railroad Culture—*www.bbcrc.org*

Adventuring by Wes Modes—*www.thespoon.com/trainhop/*
More articles and tales about adventuring, with a good section on freight hopping

WEBSITES FOR TRAVELING

CouchSurfing—*www.couchsurfing.org*
Good place to find a couch to crash on for the night

Digihitch—*www.digihitch.com*
Great hitchhiking website with info and forums, as well as people looking for and offering rides

GlobalFreeloaders—*www.globalfreeloaders.com*
Similar site to CouchSurfing

Hitchwiki—*www.hitchwiki.org*
Another good site for hitchhiking and other ways of getting around on the cheap

Squat the Planet—*http://squattheplanet.com/*
Good traveling forum site

Adventure Cycling Association—*www.adventurecycling.org*
If you're planning to get around by bike, this is a good place to start

Warmshowers—*www.warmshowers.com*
Site specifically for cyclists to find and offer places to stay for the night

WEBSITES FOR FINDING WORK

Craigslist—*www.craigslist.org*
Craigslist, the modern day's tonic

World Wide Opportunities on Organic Farms (WWOOF)—*www.wwoof.org*
The name pretty much says it all. Great resource, great people

RESOURCES FOR LIVING OFF WHAT OTHERS DON'T WANT

Freegan.info—*http://freegan.info/media-center/freeganism-in-practice/*
A hub of information for recycling other people's stuff and making it your own—from food to clothes

Freecycle—*www.freecycle.org*
A place where you can post what you need and find people who are giving stuff away. Yep, you guessed it; it's all free

GOOD BOOKS ABOUT/BY HOBOS

Black, Jack. *You Can't Win*
A real gritty and captivating autobiography by Jack Black. A tour of an America during the early 1900s that people don't talk about in fine company.

Cotton, Eddy Joe. *Hobo*
A really entertaining and no-holds-barred look at life as a modern hobo by Eddy Joe Cotton, who left home at nineteen.

Duffy, Littlejohn. *Hopping Freight Trains in America*
Considered for a long time the definitive book on train hopping.

Kerouac, Jack. *On the Road*
An American classic and cross-country adventure.
Kerouac, Jack. *The Dharma Bums*
Coming out just after *On the Road, The Dharma Bums* is not just a great tale of trains, travel, and experience, but puts you right inside the heart of the Beat movement, a real inside glimpse into the cultural start of what would become the sixties.

London, Jack. *The Road*
Collection of stories from London's days traveling in the late 1800s. Great insight into what it meant to be a hobo when the lifestyle was still coming of age.

Williams, Cliff (Oats). *One More Train to Ride: The Underground World of Modern American Hobos*
A collection of stories, music, and poems drawn from his interviews of fourteen hobos. Good, and a fast read.

Index

ABOUT THE AUTHOR

Josh Mack has worked as a painter, a carpenter working and traveling the Northeast out of an old telephone company van that refused to die, an advertising copywriter, and a freelance writer. He is also the author of *Karma 101: What Goes Around Comes Around and What You Can Do about It*. He's traveled the United States extensively, and spent a year traveling through India and Nepal by foot, train, bus, motorcycle, and the occasional *burro*. A native of Ithaca, New York, he currently lives in New York City with his wife, Alyssa, where they both pay to ride the subway.